CONWY VALLEY

160 pages of Carreg Gwalch

BEST WALKS

Editor: Llywarch ap Myrddin

Carreg Gwalch Best Walks in the Conwy Valley

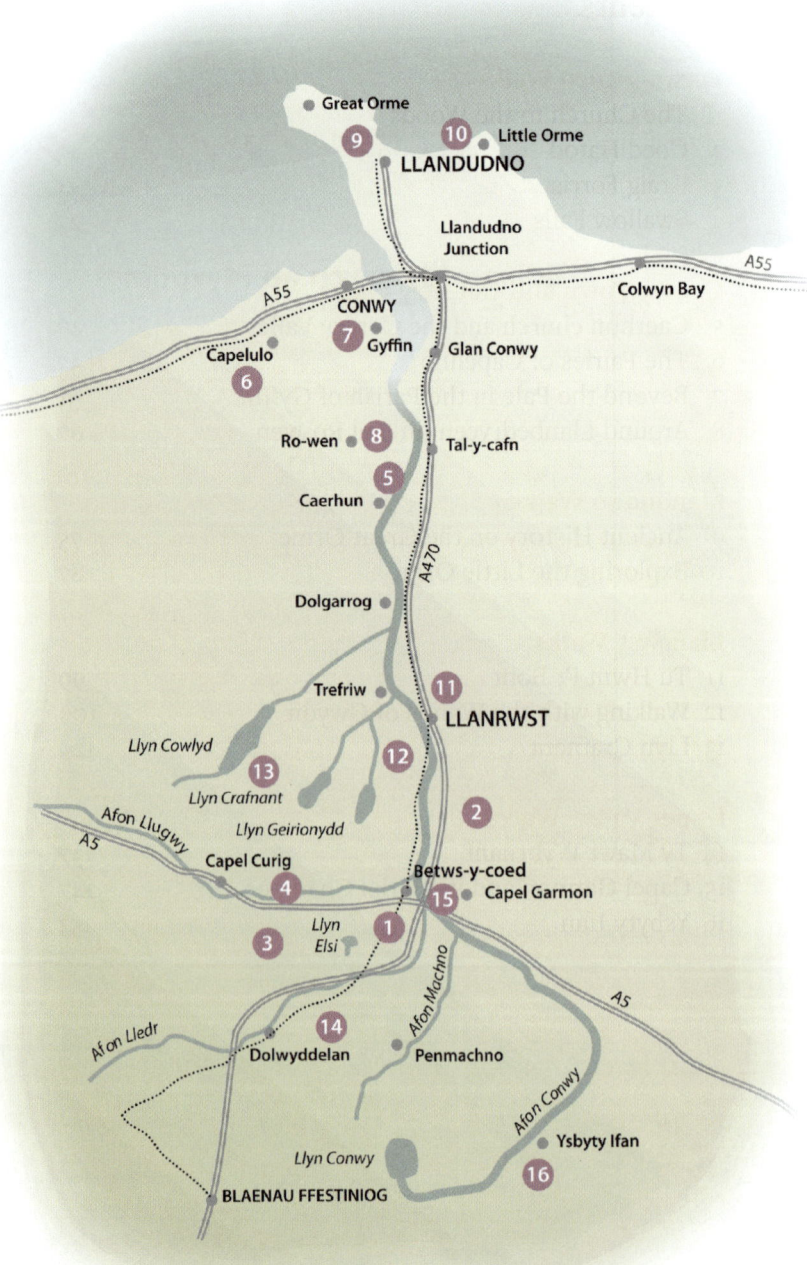

Contents

Betws-y-coed Walks
1. The Church in the Woods — 5
2. Coed Hafod — 13
3. Craig Forris — 21
4. Swallow Falls — 23

Conwy Town and Country Walks
5. Caerhun church and the Conwy Valley — 27
6. The Fairies of Capelulo — 37
7. Beyond the Pale in the Parish of Gyffin — 51
8. Around Llanbedrycennin and Ro-wen — 67

Llandudno Walks
9. Ancient History on the Great Orme — 75
10. Exploring the Little Orme — 87

Llanrwst Walks
11. Tu Hwnt i'r Bont — 99
12. Walking with the Wynns of Gwydir — 109
13. Llyn Crafnant — 129

Upper Valley Walks
14. Tŷ Mawr Wybrnant — 137
15. Capel Garmon and its Burial Chamber — 147
16. Ysbyty Ifan — 153

Trefriw
11
LLANRWST
Llyn Cowlyd
12
13
Llyn Crafnant
2
Afon Llugwy
Llyn Geirionydd
A5
Capel Curig
Betws-y-coed
4
15
Capel Garmon
Llyn
Elsi
1
3

A5
Afon Llugwy
Artist's
Wood
Miner's Bridge
Betws-y-coed
B5106
Pont-y-pair
P
Afon Conwy
Gwydir Forest
Park
Llyn
Elsi

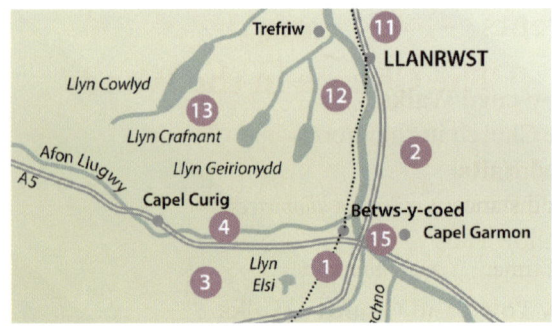

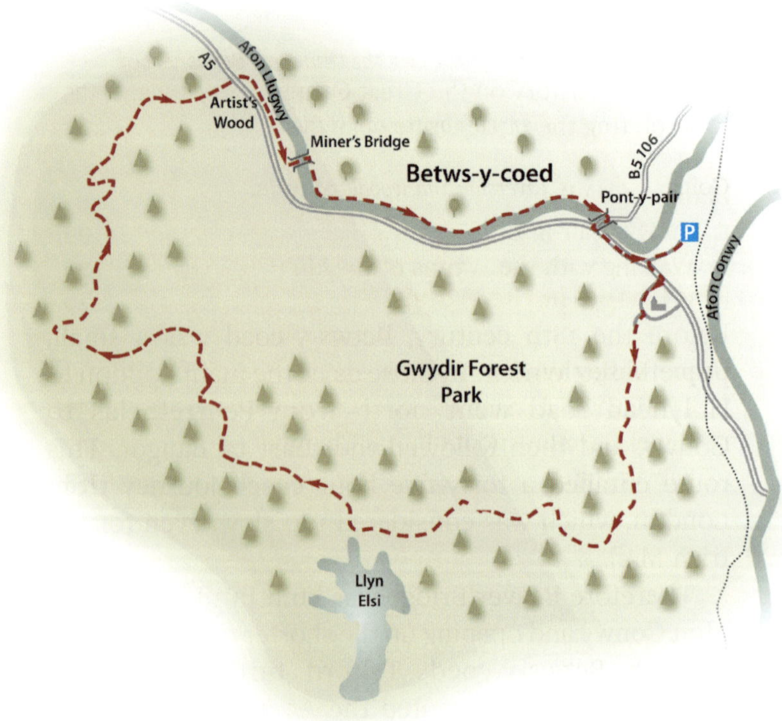

Walk 1
The Church in the Woods

Walk details
Approx distance: *4 miles/6.4 kilometres*

Approx time: *3-3½ hours*

O.S. Maps: *1:50 000 Landranger Sheet 115*
1:25 000 Explorer OL 17

Start: *Station car park, Betws-y-coed.*
Grid Ref. SH 795 566

Access: *Minor road past the church at Betws-y-coed.*

Parking: *Car park by the rail station.*

Going: *Riverside and woodland paths.*

The Chapel in the Woods

Before the 18th century, Betws-y-coed was a small, peaceful settlement. In those days, the main London to Holyhead road went north from Pentrefoelas to Conwy, and then followed the coast to Bangor. This route entailed a forty-five hour coach journey from London, which was considered too slow, even for the Irish Mail.

Therefore Beaver Bridge was built in 1803, crossing Afon Conwy and opening up the shorter route to Bangor through Betws-y-coed. Telford further improved matters when he re-routed the A5 and crossed Afon Conwy with the larger Waterloo Bridge in 1815.

Betws-y-coed began to thrive. Coaching Inns and

The old St Michael church, Betws-y-coed

the Smithy were built and the increase in traffic resulted in the village being 'discovered' as a place to visit. Its beauty was further publicised by the works of travelling artists who came to Betws-y-coed to satisfy the Victorian trend for (picturesque) pictures depicting the beauty of raw and untamed nature. Wild rivers, waterfalls and rapids crashing through wooded glens in dappled sunlight were now on a major coaching route and therefore, being accessible to both professional and amateur artists, Betws-y-coed's popularity was assured.

Then, in 1868, came the railway and Betws-y-coed was suddenly accessible to all. It was to become a resort in its own right.

A Forest, a Reservoir and a Riverside Walk
Our walk encompasses some of the beauty spots favoured by the Artists, but it is not feasible to walk to

them all for this would entail covering a considerable distance, much of it on roads.

From the centre of Betws-y-coed we climb into the forest towards Llyn Elsi. This is a reservoir that dates back to when Betws-y-coed had its own Urban District Council, the smallest such council in Britain. The lake's banks are cloaked in heather and there are fine views across towards Eryri (*Snowdonia*) generally, and Moel Siabod in particular.

The descent from the lake brings us to the A5 and Artist's Wood, a walk following Afon Llugwy through naturally regenerated beech woods. It was a popular and accessible haunt for the Victorian Artists. This will lead to Miner's Bridge. A version of this bridge was built by the miners of Rhiwddolion, a village (now deserted) that was on the Roman road known as Sarn Helen. The bridge is unusual in that one bank is much higher than the other and so the structure resembles a ladder. Afon Llugwy is now followed downstream on the opposite bank until we come to Pont-y-pair, dating from 1475. This fascinating structure is a focal point for the village, and is much photographed.

Near to the car park is a Visitor Centre, a Motor Museum and Railway Museum as well as numerous places for refreshment.

Other places that are worth visiting are: Rhaeadr Ewynnol, the name of which describes the frothy nature of the water cascading over the rocks. Some misinformed person understood the latter part of the name to be *Y Wennol*, which means Swallow, and the wrong translation is now known to a far wider public than the more picturesque original. They can be found opposite a hotel which has just as uninformed a name, and you will probably have to mingle with coach parties seeking 'a bit of nature' on the other side of the turnstile. Half a mile/800m further on, just over a bridge is Tŷ Hyll (*'the ugly house'*). It was supposedly built in one night to take advantage of the ancient laws of Hywel Dda in the 10th century. A house was considered the property of the bondman if it was completely built between sunset and sunrise and smoke was coming out of the chimney before dawn. One would suppose that such large, ill-fitting boulders would be prone to the ingress of damp. Further examination will show that the top surface of the stones are all cleverly angled outwards to repel rain, a considerable achievement working in the dark!

To the south of Betws-y-coed, the first bridge crossing Afon Conwy is Waterloo Bridge and the next is Beaver Bridge. From here a short walk up a lane from the Fairy Glen Hotel will bring you to a circular tour of the Fairy Glen itself, but there is an admission charge. You may wish to continue up the lane, for this was the old coaching route to Betws-y-coed before Telford upgraded and re-routed the road. Alternatively you can park at the junction of the B4406 with the A5 (Grid Ref. SH 811 535), walk towards Betws-y-coed along the A5 for a short distance, and then branch off to the left at a lay-by. Following this lane, that was once a major coaching route, certainly makes one realise how hazardous travelling was some two hundred years ago.

Beyond, at the first crossing point on Afon Machno, is Penmachno Mill and the Roman Bridge. This was allegedly built around AD 200, and is certainly very old for it is a packhorse bridge. Continuing past the Mill on this minor road will bring you past the Machno falls and you will continue down to Pont Lledr, built in 1468.

Walk directions

1. From the car park, cross the A5 and turn right towards the church. Turn off the main road and follow a minor road round behind the church to where a track leading up into the woods will be found, passing a barrier on the way next to the information board. Note the blue and white-topped marker post. Continue up the stony track, passing another such post and on to cross a stream by a seat and a sign to Llyn Elsi. Continue up past more posts to where the track forks. Take the right fork marked by a white-topped post. This leads to a T-junction where you turn right as marked by a white-topped post. At the next junction bear left uphill (white post) and then right at the following junction (white post). Continue up to another T-junction and follow the white post to the left, which leads to Llyn Elsi.

2. At the lakeside, turn back to the right, with the lake on your left, along a narrow path (white post) and continue up to a viewing point overlooking the lake with a stone plinth on the summit. Now ignore the path marked by the white post and take the path to the left passing the end of the lake, and follow it to the small dam. Do not cross the wooden bridge but turn right along a path parallel to the stream. This soon meets a stone road. Now turn left along the road. At a junction marked 'Hafod Las', keep left along the main

Llyn Elsi

track and then bear right at the next junction. Continue along this designated cycleway passing where another road enters from the left. Keep to this main forestry road, passing on to more open country and follow the 'S' bends downhill. You will pass a view into the valley to the west of Betws-y-coed and see the A5 road in the bottom. Continue round the hillside and on down the stone road to a junction under some power cables.

Bear right and follow the main track downhill to where it will eventually meet the A5 road.

3. Cross the road to the footpath and turn left. Soon you will come to a gap in the wall with a wooden barrier. Take this path down to the river and swing right along the river bank by the old house ruins, following it downstream through

Artist's Wood. Continue along this path, rough in places, crossing a wooden bridge to the Miner's Bridge. It is not immediately spotted, but is opposite a lone house on the A5 to your right. The path swings left and down some steps to the river.

4. Cross the bridge, which in itself is a steep climb, and turn right along the opposite bank still following the river downstream. The path will cross a ladder stile into an open riverside field and then become woods again. Continue until you come to Pont-y-pair. This you cross and turn left along the A5 through Betws-y-coed to the car park.

Originally published in
*Family Walks to Discover
North Wales*

by Anna & Graham Francis

Carreg Gwalch Best Walks in the Conwy Valley

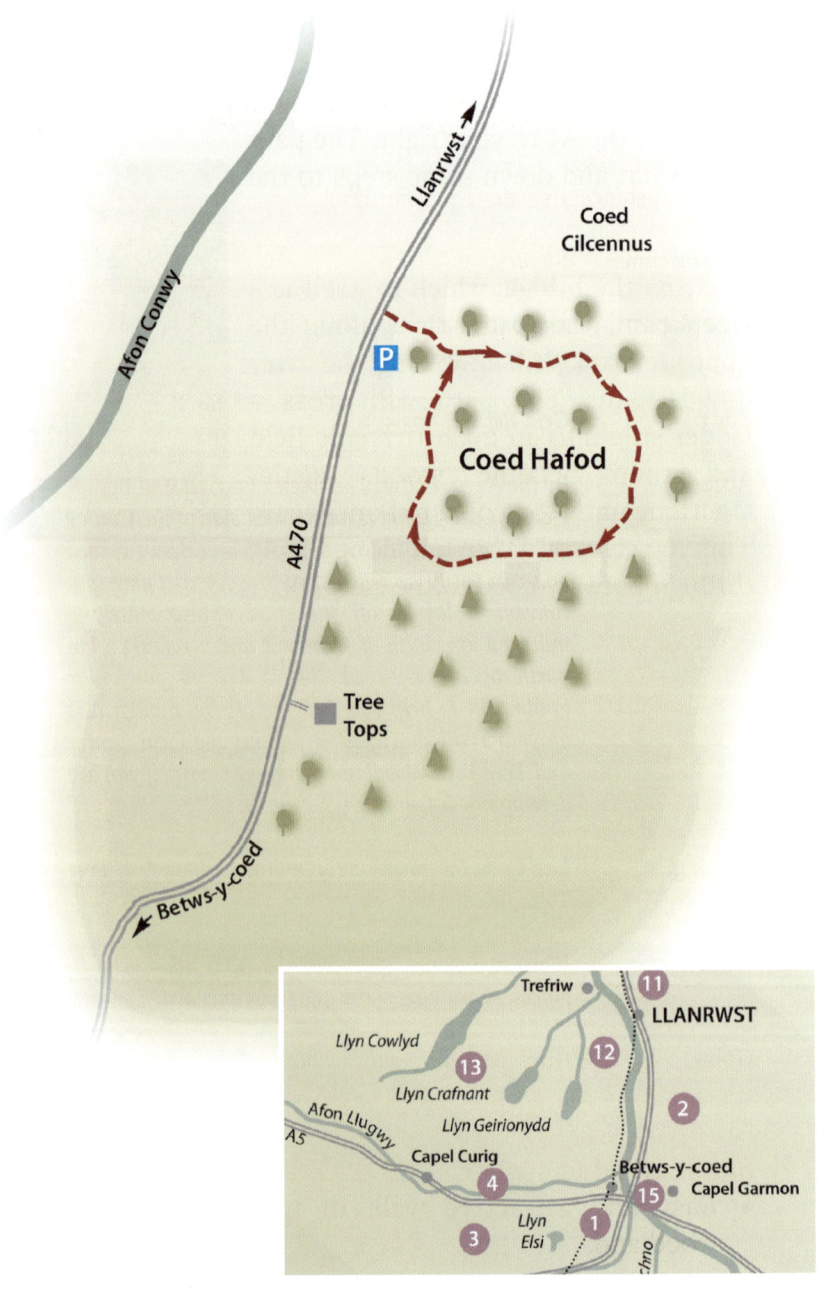

Walk 2
Coed Hafod

Walk details
Approx distance: 1½ miles/2.4 kilometres

Approx time:	1 hour
O.S. Maps:	1:50 000 *Landranger* Sheet 116 1:25 000 *Explorer* OL 17
Start:	Grid Ref. SH 805 578
Access:	By the A470, halfway between Llanrwst and Betws-y-coed. Coed Hafod is on the east side of the Conwy valley, halfway between Llanrwst and Betws-y-coed and can easily be reached on the A470. There is a convenient lay-by off the road approximately 2 miles/3.2 km south of Llanrwst and 2 miles/3.2 km north of Betws-y-coed. There are no particular landmarks to help you find the lay-by, though it is on your right shortly after passing the Field Centre and Tree Tops Woodland Climbing Centre if you are driving north from Betws-y-coed.
Parking:	Lay-by on the north side (towards Llanrwst) of Tree Tops, the tree rope centre.
Please note:	Woodland paths which can be steep and rocky in places, so walking shoes are recommended.
Going:	Forest path during the whole walk.

Site highlights
- Easy and attractive walk in mixed deciduous woodland.

- Excellent location for classic Welsh woodland birds like Pied Flycatchers, Wood Warblers and Redstarts.

Footpath meanders through Coed Hafod

Headline description
This is a beautiful area of mixed deciduous woodland, which provides easy walking on clearly signed and well-maintained footpaths. For the best birding experience, come here early on a spring morning to appreciate the dawn chorus, with Welsh woodland specialists such as Pied Flycatchers, Redstarts and Wood Warblers, as you walk amongst the Bluebells and Wood Anemones.

Walk directions
Having parked in the lay-by, over the road from Rhyd-y-Creuau farm, walk a short distance north beside the road towards Llanrwst and turn right back on yourself up the woodland path.

This beautiful deciduous woodland can be enjoyed at any time of year, but to see and hear birds, it is best walked in spring. Birdsong will be at its peak at this time of year, particularly if you make an early start to appreciate the dawn chorus! Hearing the birds singing, and looking before all the leaves are fully opened, will make it easier to locate the birds. In spring, Bluebells and Wood Anemones carpet the ground at the edges of the woodland, and in the more open clearings.

Follow the path slightly uphill and climb two stiles in quick succession over a farm track between fields. The path continues to climb slightly, then bends round to the right and levels out.

You are now entering the heart of the woodland, and the noise of the traffic on the busy A470 becomes less intrusive. This is not a walk to be rushed; walk slowly and take the time to stop and listen. You will hear birdsong all around you, but after a while you will be able to tune out the more common birds and focus in on your target birds such as Pied Flycatchers and Wood Warblers. You may come across these birds anywhere on your walk, but here is a particularly good spot for these and Garden Warblers.

At the first junction, take the footpath on your left by the walk marker and follow this uphill. After a climb, the path levels out and you reach some old stone walls. In a slight clearing here, the path forks; take the right hand path which leads you between two stone walls.

The area to the right of the path here is particularly good for Redstarts and Wood Warblers.

Walk past the stone walls and follow the path as it climbs up slightly. You will shortly reach an area of beech trees.

Look and listen carefully for Hawfinches here. You may well hear the soft 'tic' call of the bird, but as it prefers the high canopy of the trees, you may find it frustratingly hard to spot the bird itself! Nuthatches are around, and you are likely to hear and see Great Spotted Woodpeckers without too much difficulty. Lesser Spotted Woodpeckers are also present here, but are considerably harder to see, though you may hear their almost raptor-like call. In winter you may see Bramblings in this spot.

The path bends left, and then continues fairly level in a roughly southerly direction at the top of the woods. After a while you will reach the end of the deciduous woodland; the other side of a stone wall sees the start of a conifer plantation. However, the path bends and descends quite steeply along the edge of the deciduous wood. At the bottom of the hill, where the path reaches a T-junction, turn right and follow the path beside the wall. The path bends through a gap in the wall and continues heading back to the start point.

You may be aware again of the A470 on your left and be able to hear the traffic, but that doesn't disturb the wildlife. This is another good stretch of woodland for Bluebells and Wood Anemones. Song Thrushes and Robins sing loudly to defend their territories, and Pied Flycatchers can also be seen along this stretch. You may catch sight of a Goldcrest, and even Firecrests have been recorded here in the holly bushes.

Ignoring the path that comes in on the right, continue retracing your steps to where you first entered the woodland. The path bends left and descends towards the two stiles. Cross these and one more to reach the road level and walk back to the lay-by.

What to look for ...
... in spring: This really is best as a spring walk. Almost anywhere along your walk in springtime you are likely to hear and see the specialist species of Welsh woodlands: Pied Flycatchers, Redstarts, and Wood Warblers. Lesser Spotted Woodpeckers are around but very elusive – you would be lucky indeed to see one, and you may hear, even if not see, Hawfinches in the tree canopy. Garden Warblers, Willow Warblers, Chiffchaffs, Blackcaps and Tree Pipits are also to be found here.

... all year round: Nuthatches, Treecreepers and Great Spotted Woodpeckers are relatively easy to find at any time of year, particularly in the area of beech trees. Goldcrests occur in some of the lower growing holly bushes, and even Firecrests have been found here.

Where to eat
Being equidistant from Llanrwst and Betws-y-coed, you are just two

Tree Top Adventure Centre

miles in either direction from a range of cafes, pubs, restaurants and hotels to suit all appetites and budgets. You have a much wider choice of facilities in Betws-y-coed, but this attractive village can be busy at weekends and holidays.

Other information
- Parking in roadside lay-by.
- No facilities on site, nearest public toilets in either Llanrwst or Betws-y-coed.

What other sights are nearby
- Attractive riverside centres of Betws-y-coed and Llanrwst.
- Gwydir Castle (privately owned but open to the public) and Gwydir Forest.
- Tree Top Adventure Centre – outdoor activities at a unique high ropes centre available to wide range of customers. Open 7 days a week with visitor centre, licenced bar and cafe, showers, car park. www.ttadventure.co.uk
- Conwy RSPB Reserve.

Originally published in
Birds, Boots and Butties: Conwy Valley/Eastern Snowdonia

by Ruth Miller

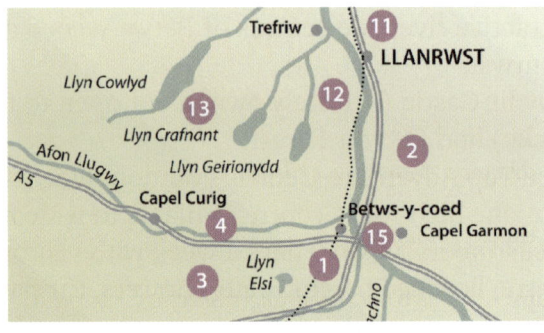

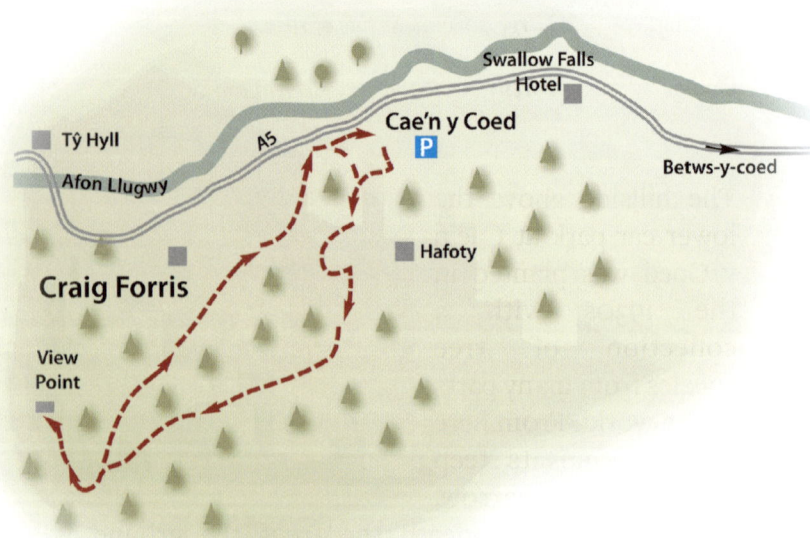

Walk 3
Craig Forris

Walk details
Approx distance: 1½ miles/2.4 kilometres

Approx time:	1 hour
O.S. Maps:	1:50 000 *Landranger Sheet 115* 1:25 000 *Explorer OL 17*
Start:	*Grid Ref. SH 763 575*
Access:	*A5 between Betws-y-coed and Capel Curig.*
Parking:	*Large car park at side of road.*
Going:	*Forestry trail and very steep at times.*

The hillside above the lower car park at Cae'n y Coed was planted in the 1930s with a collection of tree species from many parts of the world. From here the trail begins its steep ascent as a narrow, zigzag footpath. Beneath the trees the ground is carpeted with mosses, ferns and bilberries. Soon there is a brief outward view across Hafoty smallholding fields, then the climb resumes, but eases after a track. Moel Siabod is now directly ahead, framed between high larches. Further on, the woodland has been felled,

The view from Craig Forris

revealing a hollow below the road, the old Craig Forris farmhouse, which was abandoned at the turn of the century. The traditional sheltering sycamores still stand beside the old house.

A short diversion to the left reveals a matchless view of the Snowdonia skyline, before making an easy descent to the car park by the forest road.

Walk 4
Swallow Falls

Walk details
Approx distance: 2½ miles/4 kilometres

Approx time: 2½ hours

O.S. Maps: 1:50 000 *Landranger Sheet 115*
                  1:25 000 *Explorer OL 17*

Start: Grid Ref. SH 763 583

Access: *Take the narrow uphill road behind Tŷ Hyll for 1 km to reach Ty'n Llwyn car park.*

Parking: *Ty'n Llwyn car park.*

Please note: *Very dangerous at Point 3.*

Going: *Riverside forestry track, very steep in places.*

Walk directions
1. Start at Ty'n Llwyn. Walk down through a gap in the fence by the car park and follow the yellow-top markers down clear path.

2. After a sharp corner to your right, cross an old stone wall ruin. After 50m cross forest track and continue ahead downwards. On reaching another forest track take the track on your right, marked by the yellow signpost. Continue along the forest track – the Llugwy river will soon be on your right.

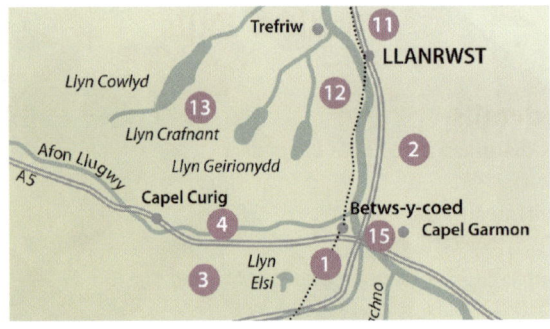

The foamy waters of 'Swallow Falls'

3. The path narrows, keep on ahead. Walk with the fence on your right. You can take a right here down the steps to see Swallow Falls, where there is a bench. Retrace your steps back up to the path and turn right to carry on with the walk.

This part of the walk is very dangerous, the fence has fallen in places, with a big drop. **Be careful!!**

4. At a fork where the fence stops take the left path. Turn left when coming to a wider path. On reaching a forest track turn right, following the markers. After 50m turn left up steps and continue upwards.

After a steep climb you can walk to a viewpoint – be careful of the steep drop.

Return to the path, go through a gap in the wall and carry on upwards back to the car park.

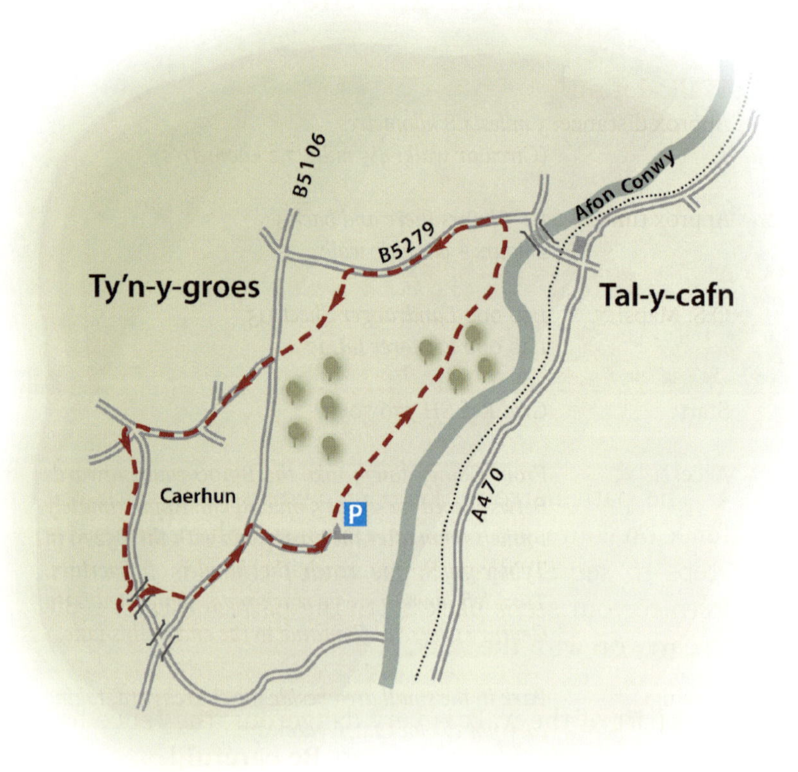

Carreg Gwalch Best Walks in the Conwy Valley

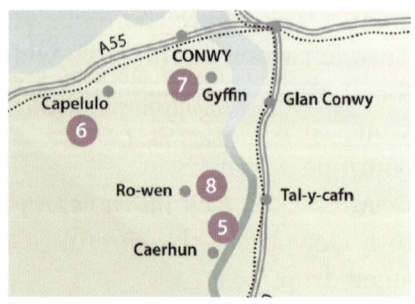

Walk 5
Caerhun church and the Conwy Valley

Walk details

Approx distance: *3 miles/4.8 kilometres*
(Circular walk: 4½ miles/7.2 kilometres)

Approx time: *1-1½ hours there and back*
2 hours – circular walk

O.S. Maps: *1:50 000 Landranger Sheet 115*
1:20 000 Explorer OL 17

Start: *Grid Ref. SH 776 704*

Access: *From Conwy town, take the B5106 south towards Betws-y-coed for about 5 miles/8 km. Approximately 1 mile/1.6 km after the crossroads with the B5279 in Ty'n-y-groes, you reach the hamlet of Caerhun. Turn left down a single track road, signposted '13th Century Church'. Continue to the end of this lane.*

Parking: *Park in the small area beside the churchyard, taking care not to block farm gateways.*

Please note: *Due to church services, parking is not allowed here on Sunday mornings. If you visit at this time, continue on the B5106 for a few hundred metres beyond the lane, where there is a larger lay-by slightly further down the hill on the left-hand side of the B-road.*

Going: *Easy walking on footpaths and country lanes.*

Caerhun church

Site highlights
- Historic church and site of Roman fort of Canovium.
- Views of Conwy valley, and the hills of Tal y Fan and Pen y Castell.
- Waders on Afon Conwy seen from Caerhun churchyard and Tal-y-cafn bridge.

Headline description
This gentle walk is set in the attractive Conwy Valley. It starts in the peaceful setting of Caerhun churchyard, which gives good views over stretches of Afon Conwy which are otherwise unreachable, an ideal spot for winter birding. The 13th century church is built on the site of Canovium Roman Fort, an auxiliary fort between Chester and Caernarfon. There are also signs of a civilian settlement, including a bathhouse by the river itself, and part of the walk follows the route of the original Roman track. The Tal-y-cafn bridge allows

good views of birds on the mudflats exposed at low tide on Afon Conwy. On the return leg, you are rewarded with a clear view of the beautiful Tal y Fan and Pen y Castell hills, which lie within the Eryri/Snowdonia National Park.

Walk directions

Start by walking into the churchyard for views overlooking Afon Conwy.

Ancient yew trees, contemporary with the 13th century church, stationed around the churchyard, are often alive with birds; keep a sharp eye open for the elusive Hawfinch in winter in particular. In early spring, snowdrops carpet the ground.

Returning to the parking area, climb the stile to your right and follow the track downhill towards the river. Go through the gate into the next field, still following the track. 150m before you reach the cottage at the riverside, leave the track and bear left to the ladder stile in the left-hand corner of the field. Walk straight across the next field towards the trees and cross the stile into the woodland.

Beech woodland is uncommon in this part of the country so it is worth taking the time to look for woodland birds. Beech trees are also the favoured habitat for Hawfinches, so look carefully for this elusive bird. You are very likely to see Pheasants as they are encouraged around here, though not if you choose the shooting season for your walk when they're likely to be lying low!

Follow the path straight through this narrow strip of mainly beech woodland and over the next stile into the field. Follow the right-hand edge of this field, with good views of Tal y Fan to your left. Pass through the gate and cross the farmyard, following the track round to the left of the large barn signalled by the yellow-top footpath sign. Continue round behind the barn and follow the track with the farmhouse on your right and farmsteading on your left. The track continues downhill and is closer to the river here.

The damp shady conditions here are ideal for Marsh Marigolds, and in spring their bright yellow flowers combine with daffodils to make this a very pretty stretch.

Follow the track until you reach some houses and the B5279. Turn right and cross the Tal-y-cafn Bridge, looking up – and downstream for waders as you do so.

This stretch of the river is tidal, and at low tide, significant areas of mud are exposed, attracting a variety of waders, gulls and the occasional Goosander. Common Sandpipers are usually regular visitors here in the summer months, while you may also see Sand Martins by the inner bank of the river where it curves left, upstream from the bridge.

Continue over the level crossing and the Tal-y-cafn pub, which serves refreshments, is on your left by the T-junction.
   For a short there-and-back walk, go back up the B5279 and retrace your steps along the track back to Caerhun church.

For a slightly longer walk, continue along the B-road as it goes uphill and then narrows. Just before reaching the houses of Ty'n-y-groes, take the footpath on the left to cut off the corner. Go through the kissing gate marked by the footpath sign into the field, and bear right round to the next stile. Cross this next field, keeping to the left-hand side of the field edge.

In summer, this is a stunning area for wild flowers and butterflies, including Tortoiseshells, Red Admirals and Peacocks.

Climb the stile out onto the B5106. From here, it is a short walk back along the road to Caerhun.

For those wishing to walk further, cross over the B road and follow the country lane on the right-hand side of the house towards Ro-wen. Follow along this to the end of the lane.

In summer, check the hedgerows and telephone wires as you go for Greenfinches and Goldfinches. Spotted Flycatchers have been seen here. Blackberries and hazelnuts occur along here in autumn.

Turn right and enjoy the views down the Conwy valley as you walk down the lane towards the hamlet of Pontwgan. Turn left here over the road bridge crossing Afon Ro.

Pass Mill Cottage and climb the stile on your left, marked by the footpath sign, into the field. Keeping with the hedge on to your left drop down to the next stile beside the trees and cross into the water meadow by the river, enjoying the seats thoughtfully provided here. Cross the next four stiles keeping the river on your left.

Keep your eyes peeled for Dippers and Grey Wagtails on this clear, rocky little stream. Himalyan Balsam, an attractive though unfortunately pervasive invader, has also reached even this secluded stretch of water.

When you reach the fifth stile and the farm lane, turn left to where it joins the B5106. Turn left, walk up past the cemetery and turn right into the lane leading back to Caerhun church.

Just before you reach the church, where two oak trees straddle the lane, you can quite clearly see the embankment demarcating the area of the Roman Fort of Canovium.

What to look for ...
... in spring/summer: You are likely to hear and see warblers such as Willow Warblers, Chiffchaffs and Blackcaps in the willows along Afon Ro and beside Afon Conwy, while you may be lucky and see Spotted Flycatchers along your walk.

... in autumn: Look out for Redwings and Fieldfares passing through, particularly around any berried trees.

... in winter: Caerhun churchyard is one of the regular sites in northern Wales to see Hawfinches in winter. Check the tall trees along the road to the church, and pines from outside the churchyard. They may also be

Afon Conwy near Caerhun

seen in the stretch of woodland you walk through, where they may be attracted by the beech trees. From the churchyard, you can look down onto Afon Conwy where gulls and geese collect on the shallows and banks. Look out for Herring, Common and Black-headed Gulls, and you may be lucky enough to see a Mediterranean Gull. Greylag and Canada Geese gather here. You may see Wigeon, Teal and Goldeneye on the river here, and nearer Tal-y-cafn bridge. Dippers can often be seen on Afon Ro.

... all year round: The churchyard is a great place to see Goldfinches, Greenfinches and Chaffinches in good numbers. Goldcrests also occur in the ancient yew trees here. You will frequently trip over both male and female Pheasants in the beech wood and you may hear and see Jays too. Down on the river, you should see Mute Swans, Mallards, and Red-breasted

Hawfinch

Mergansers and Goosanders, and Common Sandpipers have been regularly seen by the Tal-y-cafn Bridge. Grey Wagtails can be seen on the small rushing Afon Ro all year. Keep an eye open for rarities that can occur at any time here. Sharp eyes have seen not only Otters but also a White Stork on Afon Conwy by Tal-y-cafn bridge!

Where to eat

At the time of writing, the café and shop at Tal-y-cafn were closed until further notice. The Groes Inn between Ty'n-y-groes and Conwy offers high standard inn food. Alternative refreshments can be found in the tearoom at the National Trust Bodnant Gardens, 10 minutes' drive away from Caerhun church. Return in your car along the B5106 towards Conwy. Turn right at Ty'n-y-groes onto the B5279 to Tal-y-cafn. At the main road, by the Tal-y-cafn pub, turn left onto the A470 towards Colwyn Bay. After ½ mile/0.8 km, turn right where signposted at the top of the hill for the National Trust Bodnant Gardens. The tearoom is open seven days a week from 10 a.m. to 5 p.m. from March to October, and 10 a.m. to 4 p.m. in the first half of November. It is closed the rest of the year.

Other information

- Parking by Caerhun church and nearby lay-bys. Large car park at Tal-y-cafn Hotel.
- Toilets at Tal-y-cafn Hotel for customers only.

Afon Conwy and Tal-y-cafn bridge

What other sights are nearby?
- Historic walled town of Conwy and castle.
- Conwy RSPB Reserve.
- Village of Betws-y-coed and the Gwydir Forest.
- National Trust Bodnant Gardens.
- Bodnant Food Centre.
- The nearby Groes Inn claims to be the oldest pub in Wales.

Originally published in
Birds, Boots and Butties: Conwy Valley/Eastern Snowdonia

by Ruth Miller

Carreg Gwalch Best Walks in the Conwy Valley

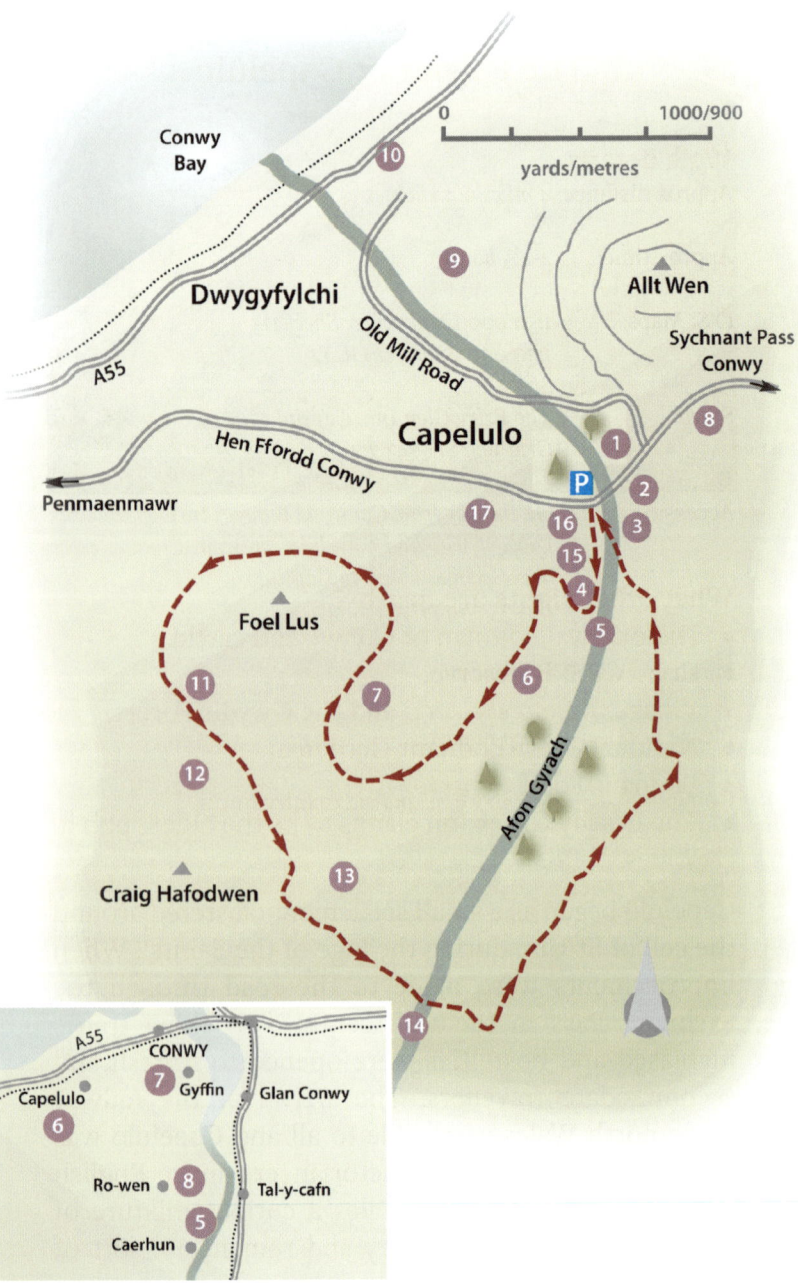

Walk 6
The Fairies of Capelulo

Walk details

Approx distance: *4 miles/6.4 kilometres*

Approx time: 2-2½ *hours*

O.S. Maps: 1:50 000 *Landranger Sheet 115*
1:20 000 *Explorer OL 17*

Start: *The Fairy Glen Inn, Capelulo*
Grid Ref. SH 743 766

Access: *On the A55 from Conwy to Bangor, turn off towards Dwygyfylchi and Capelulo; or from Conwy, cross over Sychnant Pass to Capelulo.*
Bus 75 – approx 4 a day.

Parking: *On roadside.*

Please note: *Steep in parts.*

Going: *Country lane and old country tracks.*

Capelulo began as a small settlement clustered around the cell of St Ulo, during the 'Age of the Saints'. When improvements were made to the road through the Sychnant Pass in the 18th century, coaching traffic increased and hostelries were opened to refresh and accommodate travellers. The arrival of the railway made north Wales accessible to all and Capelulo was keen to cash in. In the Victorian era most English visitors expected to find Wales a curious mixture of picturesque scenery, mystery and romance: a sort of

Dwygyfylchi – at the starting point

primitive fairyland. Capelulo, with its welcoming inns, superb setting and secluded Fairy Glen offered a magical experience.

Walk directions and Points of Interest
From the Fairy Glen Inn (2), glance across the road at the small copse (1), alongside the river.

1. Ulo's Chapel or cell is thought to have been somewhere here, above the bridge, amongst trees, on the banks of Afon Gyrach. One of many wandering Celtic missionaries St Ulo would have relished this quiet, sheltered spot with all the elements necessary for life at-hand. This 6th and 7th century is known in Wales as the 'Age of the Saints' when many similar Christian missionaries travelled the land. In this era the Celtic Church embraced the simple principles of Christianity, without the centralisation, hierarchies and corruption that characterised the Roman Church.

2. The Fairy Glen Inn was built in 1772 to serve the coaches travelling over the Sychnant Pass and was originally known as the Cross Keys. When long-distance coaching declined with the growth of the railways, in the mid-19th century, trade actually increased. On summer days the inn's forecourt was often packed with four-in-hand tourist coaches on day trips from Conwy, Llandudno and Colwyn Bay. The horse-drawn trip over the Sychnant Pass combined the picturesque with the dramatic and included just a hint of danger. A refreshment stop here was often combined with a stroll along our proposed route into the Fairy Glen. In 1898 the Marston Brewery, Burton-on-Trent purchased the Cross Keys and with an eye to increasing its tourist appeal in 1909 changed the name to 'The Fairy Glen'.

Facing the Fairy Glen Inn turn right and then first left up the lane that runs alongside the end of the building. After 20 yards (18m) or so, you notice a house (3), on the left, with its gable end alongside the lane.

3. This route down to the Fairy Glen was so popular with Victorian tourists that the householder here decided to open up as a guesthouse and refreshment room. Just above the two gable windows, a huge sign, running the entire width of the building used to announce, 'Mineral Waters & Accommodation for Cyclists'.

Continue until you reach the far end of the last house on the right. Pausing outside 'Woodpecker Cottage' notice a metal lamp-post-like pole (4) on the right of the lane.

4. It is hard to believe that such an attractve little item of street-furniture serves the humble function of venting the drains to prevent a build-up of noxious and possibly explosive gases. This is a small architectural gem; the material is cast iron and the makers, William Macfarlane & Company, of Glasgow.

Continue ahead for about 100 yards (90m), until you come to a gate (5) with a much-rebuilt house, Foxhole, ahead. Do not go through the gate!

5. Beyond the gate lies 'The Fairy Glen – Capelulo's greatest tourist attraction'. Baddeley and Ward's 1892 guide book described it as 'a charming little dell containing a succession of small cascades, of which the two chief ones are near the top. Crossing and re-crossing the stream, we gain delightful peeps through the abundant foliage which overhangs it – none the less pleasing from their intermittent character'. Alice Thomas Ellis was brought up nearby and claims, 'The fairies of the glen were . . . creatures of an English imagination, little things with gossamer wings and acorn cups for hats. Welsh fairies – the *Tylwyth Teg* – more resembled the human race: miniature people with miniature horses and dogs. They were richly dressed in red and green and were ruled over by Gwyn ap Nudd. On the whole they were well disposed towards humans and would perform household tasks on receipt of a bowl of milk and some bread . . . they lived in more remote places than the glen, up on the hills and even under them'. In 19th century rural Wales many accepted the reality of the *Tylwyth Teg* but if English visitors preferred their own cute, romanticised version why not sell it back to them? So this 'Fairy

Glen' was advertised as their natural home, for surely any free-flying fairy would prefer to settle here than in Manchester or Liverpool. For more than fifty years, by handing over a fee of three pence at Foxhole cottage, you were permitted to stroll amidst the enchanted scenery beyond the gate. Before the war a pair of maiden aunts lived in the cottage, which smelled of wood-smoke and baking, and they served bread and butter and tea and Welsh cakes to visitors. They had a pet lamb called Megan, but they have all gone now. The gate is locked and the new owners do not wish to share their delightful glen with anybody else. The fairies have departed in disgust.

Turn back to ascend the path. Following the path, you soon bear left above a small mountain cottage where a magnificent vista opens up before you. Continuing to bear left you follow the main path, which runs alongside a dry-stone wall as the gradient levels out (6).

6. There are some beautiful examples of dry-stone walling on this area of moorland and rough grazing. The walls generally demarcate areas of improved grazing and most date back to the 18th century.

Looking over to the right you should see two stone farmhouses (7), Ffridd-y-foel and Bwthyn Llwyd.

7. Bwthyn Llwyd, on the right, is a most impressive old farmhouse whilst Ffridd-y-foel appears to be a Johnny-come-lately barn conversion. This is almost the reverse of the truth, for Ffridd-y-foel stood here, alone for two centuries before being joined by Bwthyn Llwyd. Ffridd-y-foel was erected in the 18th century by squatters, who cleared, improved and walled-off a section of moorland, despite the ever-present threat of eviction. Towards the end of the 19th century this became the childhood home of Huw T. Edwards, an interesting politician who acquired fame as a passionate advocate of Socialism, Welsh Nationalism and trade union rights. This place left an abiding impression on Huw and he would often recall the hours spent walking the hills with his mother, who died here when he was still only a boy.

Continue to follow the old cart track, which continues south-west, before curving around and then turning north-east to pass just the other side of those two farms. Soon you pass the two houses and heading north-east you reach the crest of the hill, with a magnificent view up the Sychnant Pass (8).

8. Sychnant Pass is now a very minor route for traffic through northern Wales but in the years before Telford improved the coastal route, this was the more attractive option. The old route along the headland was notoriously precipitous. At low tide coaches could sometimes travel over the sands but when this was impossible travellers would either endure delay or

have their coach dismantled and carried around the narrow headland path by footmen. Travellers along the headland route were occasionally so troubled by the sheer drop that they preferred to be blindfolded and led along the path by stout-hearted companions. Improvements to the Sychnant Pass road in the 18th century enabled the coaches to abandon the difficulties of the coastal route and Capelulo expanded rapidly to serve the traffic. The opening of the new, improved coastal route in 1826 led to a decline in Capelulo's fortunes for a while but, before long, serious travellers were replaced by those travelling for pleasure and seekers of sublime scenery.

Bearing right, continue on the main, level path for 500 yards (455m) before pausing to survey Dwygyfylchi, notice the following features: a large, painted Georgian mansion (9), in the distance, with a caravan park to the fore and further west, the A55 road tunnels (10).

9. Pendyffryn was built in the late 18th century for George Thomas Smith, a member of a notable Durham dynasty. Smith did much to develop local agriculture and was personally responsible for the introduction of the turnip to Dwygyfylchi! In 1854 Pendyffryn was acquired by a Manchester solicitor, Samuel Dukinfield Darbishire, who greatly enlarged the house, both to cater for his large family and also to 'impress the natives', for he was yet another affluent English Victorian with squirarchical ambitions. Darbishire was a prominent Liberal and it was on his invitation that William Ewart Gladstone first visited the area. The Darbishires soon began acquiring interests in local quarries and on 1 January, 1878 they gained complete

control of Penmaenmawr's Graiglwyd Quarry and installed Samuel's son, Charles Henry, as manager.

10. The view of the Penmaen-bach headland from here shows just what a formidable barrier it posed to traffic along the coast, and illustrates why it was thought at one time that even the problems of a route through the Sychnant Pass might be more easily overcome. Telford's 1826 route cut a narrow shelf around the headland that still exists, but is by-passed by the A55 that penetrates the headland via two tunnels: the 565 foot (170m) long eastbound tunnel was opened in 1932, the westbound sixty years later.

Following the path around the hill a magnificent view over Penmaenmawr soon appears, and then notice, on the left, a small cave (11).

11. This 'cave' only runs back about 30 feet (9m) into the hill and is not really a natural cave but rather a 19th century 'mining level' or trial extraction.

After another 300 yards (270m) you notice two curious stone pillars (12) astride the footpath ahead.

12. These pillars mark the creation and public opening of this 'Jubilee Path' on 23 June, 1888. Originally planned as the 'Foel Lus Path' it came to be linked with the 1887 Jubilee of Queen Victoria and was popularly renamed. Foel Lus is the name of the hill which the path circumscribes. The contractor Joseph Jones, and his two assistants, completed the path in four months using only picks and shovels at a cost of only £50, with an extra £5 for building these two pillars!

Pass between the pillars and follow the path, which bears left and begins to ascend. As you continue you'll notice a stone carved to show the many paths of the area, be careful not to turn off to the left unless you wish to complete another lap of Foel Lus! Soon you'll notice a junction in the path continue right on a gentle gradient. You should spot another old Farm, Tyn-y-ffrith as the gradient levels out (13).

13. Tyn-y-ffrith was the home of Huw T. Edwards' paternal grandparents. His grandfather toiled for hours here with his spade to create a little garden from the barren, rocky earth whilst his grandmother would roam the moors collecting wool from the gorse bushes to spin and knit into clothes for the family. Besides Huw's father, four other Edwards children were born here, three girls and another boy. One of those paternal aunties, for many years, owned and ran the 'Fairy Glen Inn', down in the village.

Go through the first kissing gate and continue for about 100 yards before turning left through a farm gate. Follow the North Wales Path down to a footbridge over a stream; pause here (14).

14. This area is known as Waen Gyrach, but its unprepossessing name and appearance belie its former importance. Well into the 19th century peat was dug from the wetter areas to be dried and used as a fuel by everyone, except the wealthy who could afford to burn coal. The drier slopes were cultivated in the Middle Ages and traces of medieval furrows and field patterns can still be seen when the sun and the bracken permit. The remains of earlier hut platforms can also be discerned, but are not easy to spot.

Continuing south-east there is a large abandoned farmstead hidden behind the dry stone walls, known in the 19th century as 'Half-Way House'. Turn left here and follow the North Wales Path north-east. After about 600 yards (550m) you come alongside stone walls, enclosing fields, on the left and soon reach a junction of several tracks with a rocky outcrop. At the junction you'll see Maen Esgob, above you on the right and a small derelict single-storey cottage beyond the wall on the left. See if you can discern the prehistoric hut platform cut from the southern slope of Maen Esgob. Turn left at the junction following the path by the dry stone wall, continue downhill before walking on

past the lovely old farmstead, Pen-ffordd-goch, on the left. Continue down the green road, which passes between lovely stone walls on either side. Keep to the left as the path soon begins to descend steeply. Just before you reach the valley floor the path takes a sharp right-hand, hairpin bend and then as you descend you are looking directly at an attractive stone house (15), situated alongside the river.

15. This is Riverstones, which occupies the site of an old carding mill. Carding, or combing, wool disentangles and straightens the fibres in preparation for spinning. Originally it was done by hand using teasels or cards studded with wire pins but in 1775 Richard Arkwright made a breakthrough with mechanical carding. Water-powered carding mills made their first appearance in northern Wales in 1789 and Capelulo carding mill began here a decade later and continued in operation throughout most of the 19th century.

Turn right, away from Riverstones, continue across the river and back down into the village. Turn left at the main road, pause outside the Dwygyfylchi (16) public house and glance over at the Austrian restaurant (17).

16. 'Y Dwygyfylchi' was the 'Dwygyfylchi Hotel' in the 19th century although before 1880 it was the 'Horseshoe' tavern and is still known locally as 'Y Bedol'. The original name was a reference to the blacksmith shop that also operated here for many years, in conjunction with the hotel's coaching trade. Coach horses noticing the Sychnant Pass looming up ahead must have been greatly relieved to realise they were being reined-in here and given assistance by extra horses hired out by the hotel for that very purpose. Despite the 1880 name-change the hotel, under Ellen Evans, still advertised itself as mainly, 'Commercial and Posting'. The hotel's later name touches on a long running debate about the nomenclature of this area. Although Capelulo is a very old name, the official name of the parish was Dwygyfylchi. Nowadays the settlement nearer the sea and clustered around the old parish church of St Gwynan's is usually referred to as Dwygyfylchi and this area called Capelulo, but there is is no clear demarcation and not much consistency. In May 1901 a terrible tragedy occurred here. Despite discouragement the landlord's little two-year-old son, Charlie Woodhouse, was fond of igniting matches that he discovered in the bar. One Tuesday night, about half an hour after Maggie Benjamin, Charlie's nurse, had put him to bed at six o'clock, she heard terrible screams. Rushing up to his bedroom she discovered Charlie sitting up with the bedclothes and his nightshirt on fire. Although Maggie managed to extinguish the flames with her apron and despite Doctor Jenkins' prompt arrival, little Charlie died at midnight.

17. In Victorian times the present Austrian Restaurant served as the 'Nantyglyn Tea Rooms', run by the Misses Quixley and Barrie, who offered visitors, 'Teas, home made cakes, scones and jams'.

Originally published in
Walks from Conwy

by Christopher Draper

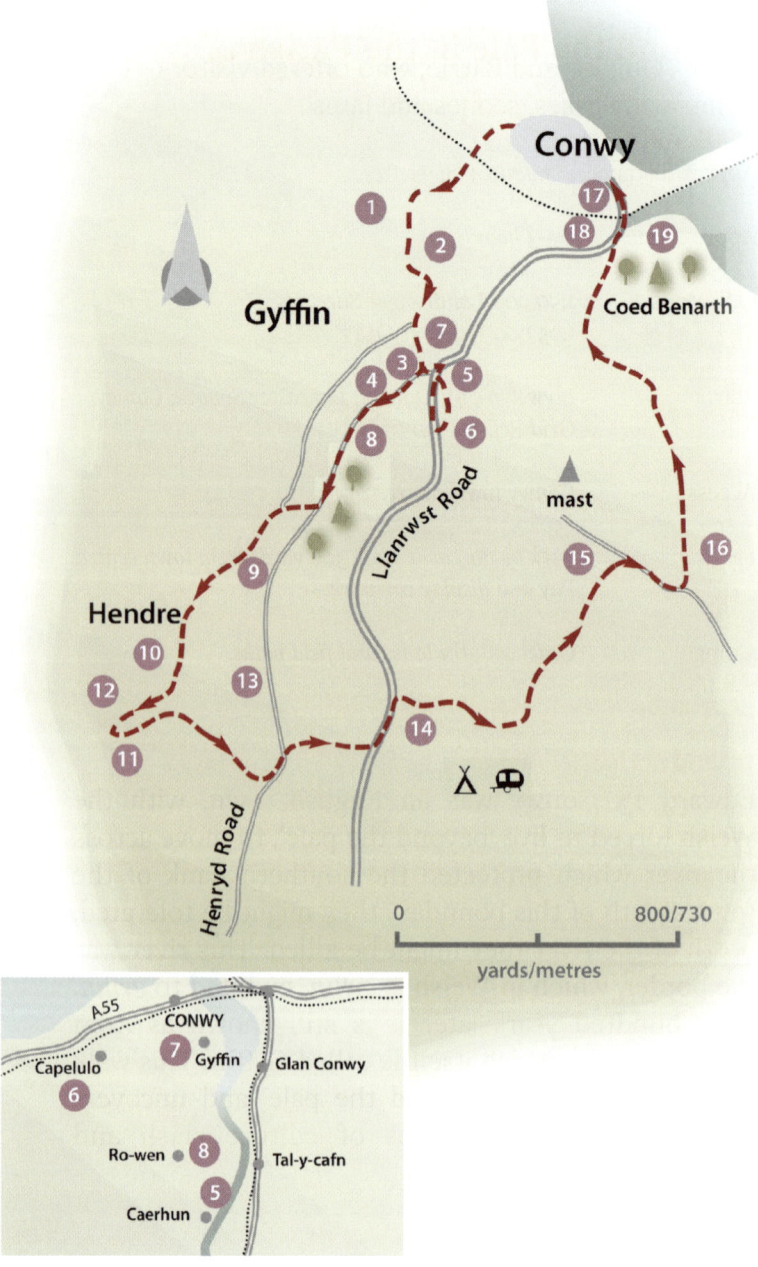

Walk 7
Beyond the Pale in the Parish of Gyffin

Walk details

Approx distance: *4 miles/6.4 kilometres*

Approx time: 2½-3 *hours*

O.S. Maps: 1:50 000 *Landranger Sheet 115*
1:25 000 *Explorer OL17*

Start: *Llywelyn's Monument, Lancaster Square, Conwy. Grid Ref. SH 781 776*

Access: *Conwy town centre.*

Parking: *Park by the castle wall, 300 yards from town centre. Pay and display car park.*

Going: *Quiet country lanes and field paths.*

Introduction

Edward I's Conwy was an English town, with the Welsh forced to live 'beyond the pale', to move across the river which protected the southern flank of the town. South of this boundary they might be tolerated, north of the river they might be killed. This river was the border, which in Welsh is *cyffin*, mutated to *gyffin*. Nine hundred years later it is still known as Afon Gyffin, and the parish itself is called Gyffin. This walk explores the parish 'beyond the pale' and uncovers more recent repercussions of culture clash and exclusivity.

Conwy castle from Gyffin

The Walk and Points of Interest

From Llywelyn's monument, walk north-east along Bangor Road. Once through the walls turn left along Mount Pleasant, then right, ascending Sychnant Pass road for 100 yards (90m). Turn left along the path by the footpath (1) sign.

1. Bryn Corach was built as a private house, in an attractive 'Scots-Baronial meets Conwy Castle' style of architecture. Since 1913 it has been owned and run by the Holiday Fellowship. HF grew out of the movement to provide access to the countryside for city-dwellers who had been increasingly deprived of the joys of nature by the relentless march of Victorian industrialisation. The founder of HF was T. A. Leonard, a non-conformist minister from Lancashire. Known as the 'father of the

open-air movement', he began by organising holiday schemes as an extension of his church's rambling club. He formed the Co-Operative Holidays Association' in 1891 and the Holiday Fellowship in 1913. Leonard personally chose Bryn Corach as a holiday centre and headquarters but was supported by an equally determined and idealistic committee, which included the influential Tolstoyan, Percy Redfern. The idealistic companionship offered by the Fellowship soon attracted progressive figures, like Bernard Shaw, to stay at Bryn Corach but when war broke out in 1914 the HF commitment to international friendship and peace was resented by local 'jingos'. Armed men were constantly banging on the front door and accusing Bryn Corach residents of flashing torches in an attempt to communicate with the enemy. The authorities were also determined to 'get Bryn Corach' but couldn't manage to prove anything until one day the dried fruit ration for three other holiday centres was delivered here by mistake. Leonard and Miss Brothers, the manageress of Bryn Corach were both summoned to appear at Conwy Police Court, prosecuted for 'hoarding food' and fined £10! Not all Conwy residents were antagonistic and many admired HF's generosity in housing Belgian refugees. The idealism continues and holiday fellowship is still available at Bryn Corach.

Continue through the metal gate and down the lane, which curves to the left and passes a short terrace of houses (2), before joining St Agnes Road, where you turn right.

2. These houses were erected in the hollow of a worked-out Victorian quarry. Stone was extracted

from here in the 1870s to consolidate and repair Conwy castle's Bakehouse Tower, courtesy of Francis G. Jones (1816-1889), the owner of the Bryn Corach Estate.

Continue as the road bears left, cross at the school sign and follow the footpath on the right as it descends the bank, crosses a metal footbridge and arrives at an ancient church (3) and churchyard (4).

3. The foundation of St Benedict's church is a bit of a mystery. The most plausible theory is that it was built in the early 13th century by the Cistercian monks of Aberconwy to serve local people whilst they reserved their abbey chapel mainly for their own use and for the devotions of their illustrious guests. It is possible, however, that the monks merely rededicated an existing church here or even that Gyffin church was built to serve the local Welsh population only after they had been expelled from Aberconwy by Edward I. If the monks did indeed build this church, it seems logical that it was dedicated to that great founder of Latin monasticism, Saint Benedict, but even here it is not so straight-forward as the Cistercians more usually dedicated their churches to Mary. Whatever the details of its foundation, by the 15th century it was already considered necessary to extend the church to cater for local people who were still excluded from town life and worship. Yet even the extensive Victorian 'improvements' of 1858 haven't entirely destroyed the ancient character of St Benedict's. Inside there is an extremely unusual 15th century painted celure, or canopy, whilst outside the porch is especially interesting. The attractive timber frame of the porch is

St Benedict's church at Gyffin

14th century, whilst the 13th century memorial stone set into the porch's left flank provides another intriguing mystery. This slightly tapering memorial stone, which can be viewed from the outside through the wooden mullions, seems to bear the inscription: HIC IACAT LLYWELYN AP IORWERTH. Could this be part of the gravestone of the founder of Aberconwy salvaged by loyal Welshmen and women when Edward ordered his body be removed from Conwy?

4. There are several other monuments scattered around St Benedict's churchyard that are worth seeking out. A large, slate table-top stone marking a family grave, behind the church, includes a memorial to 'Owen Williams, engineer of the Mail Steamer *Inca* in the Pacific Ocean who died at Tobogo (*sic*) on 29 September, 1859, aged 28'. Near the church porch, to the east of the path lie two gardeners, Richard Owen and Hugh Roberts, who worked at Benarth Hall, of

which you will hear more later. Under the branches of the large tree near the gate, to the west of the path, lies Elizabeth, wife of Thomas Williams, of the Foresters' Arms, Gyffin, which we will visit after I first explain how just over a century ago this churchyard achieved a certain notoriety. It began at 3.45 p.m. on Saturday 3 May, 1890 as the funeral procession of William Williams passed the spot where you are now standing. As the 'venerable white-haired, surpliced Rector Thomas Ellis entered the church, book in hand' the following mourners and coffin-bearers wheeled off to the left and ignoring the absence of the rector proceeded to lower the deceased into an open grave attended by a Welsh Wesleyan Minister. 'Suddenly becoming aware that no-one was following him the Rector rushed out of the church shouting.' Amidst the tears and hymn singing of the mourning family at the graveyard, the Gyffin rector who was a Conwy curate, and the Wesleyan minister began haranguing each other. The rector refused to allow the rites of the Wesleyan Conference to take place and the deceased was eventually laid to rest without any formal funeral service taking place, or any memorial stone being erected. In the ensuing publicity the rector claimed that the deceased hadn't been entitled to be buried in Gyffin as he had lived in Conwy parish, but this had not disqualified others from burial here. The real explanation is more complex for 'The Gyffin Burial Sensation' was but a single, particularly public and dramatic skirmish in a long-running and widespread battle between the established church and non-conformity.

Leave the churchyard through the main gate, turn left and when you reach the Llanrwst Road, cross to the tiny house

(5) on the opposite corner. Then ascent Llanrwst Road to the first house (6) before descending again, continuing across the road and over the bridge to the chip shop (7).

5. Turnpike Cottage has a stone set into the front gable that records its erection in 1930, during the reign of King William IV. The resident toll-collector was responsible for collecting the fees from travellers along this section of the Caernarfonshire Turnpike Road, which led from Llanrwst to Pwllheli. This was officially listed as 'gate number 2', with Gwydir, near Llanrwst as 'number 1'. The Trust didn't actually operate the gates themselves, preferring to lease them out, on an annual basis, to the highest bidder. The greatest annual amount ever collected in tolls here amounted to £108, in 1850, when John Hughes was the resident collector. The standard tolls charged were 2d. each for non-draught horses, 10d. per score of cattle in droves whilst pigs, sheep and geese were charged at 5d. a score. In 1882 the Trust expired on the adoption of the road by the local authority, all tolls ceased and the tollhouse and gate were sold off. The house fetched £80 before being resold to Robert Rowlands, the miller.

6. Notice the blank plaque which adorns the front wall above the door. A hundred years ago this bore the name of the Foresters' Arms (remember the gravestone reference?), for this was the village inn. The metal trapdoor leading down to the old beer-cellar can still be seen at street level, to the left of the front door, and the old brew-house remains in the back yard but the licence was withdrawn almost a century ago. Local opinion traces this misfortune back to the time of

Queen Victoria's funeral in 1901. The local authority asked all local businesses to close for the day as a mark of respect, but the Foresters' are believed to have been the only public house in Britain to have remained open and so lost their licence as a consequence! Unfortunately the truth is more routine, the Foresters' operated until 1903 and was eventually closed down because it offered limited facilities to bona fide travellers but rather unlimited facilities to drunks! The landlord simply ran a disorderly house, brawling was a speciality, and his licence was withdrawn as a result.

7. This was Gyffin corn mill, powered by water flowing from a pond at the rear, now filled in. Water was delivered via a long mill-race that branched off Afon Gyffin, upstream. The mill pond was contained by a mill-dam and crossed by a little bridge that originally carried the footpath that you previously followed to reach the church. The miller's house stands between the chip shop and Afon Gyffin.

Retrace your steps to the church gate before continuing along Henryd Road for 400 yards (360m) until you reach the old stone-built rectory (8), on the left.

8. This impressive residence was the home of the Reverend Thomas Robert Ellis of 'Burial Scandal' fame. Ellis was appointed to Gyffin parish as a curate in 1852 and formally appointed as Rector on 19 January, 1953. He was succeeded by Robert Jones in 1898. The Reverend Jones had thirteen children and his relatives always considered that the Bishop of Bangor offered him this situation as the large rectory seemed particular suitable for accommodating his ever

increasing family! In 1925 Gyffin lost the status of maintaining its own rector and the rectory was subsequently sold off and converted to accommodate holidaymakers.

After a further 400 yards (360m) you reach a lone house, on the right, where you descend three steps and follow a footpath over a footbridge. Bear left and on reaching the road turn left and continue for 200 yards (180m) to Tyddyn Melus (9), a white painted cottage on the left.

9. Tyddyn Melus is a delight, a largely original 18th century cottage of a type that was once common in north Wales. Notice the huge, characteristic projecting corner boulders.

Continuing in the same direction you soon reach a long terraced building alongside a T-junction (10). Continue ahead for another 200 yards (180m) to Hen Bodidda (11), on the left with a more modern farmhouse Henllys (12), on the right.

10. A century ago these buildings contained the blacksmith shop of Jabez Jones. Jabez learned the craft from Thomas, his father, a native of Llanrhos. Later in this walk I will point out an example of their Victorian handiwork.

11. Bodidda was built around 1550 by Hugh Stodart but within a hundred years it had passed into the ownership of the Owen family, with whom it is usually associated. The building was once one of the major houses of the area and although it has declined in importance something of its former status is signalled

by the presence of the bell suspended in the gable end. This indicates an establishment employing a large number of farmhands who would be rung in from their widely distributed tasks in the fields at meal times.

12. Henllys, originally Halesfield, makes an interesting contrast with Bodidda. Almost three hundred and fifty years younger, it was built more as a gentleman's country residence rather than a functional farmhouse. The prominent monkey-puzzle tree is a period sign of social pretension. Trees were traditionally planted to provide fruit and timber and shade for animals, or windbreaks for farmhouses. A monkey-puzzle announces that the owner has interests above such mundane concerns, sophisticated and exotic taste and is, in a word, a gentleman. Sadly maintaining social pretension can be stressful and in 1928 led to terrible consequences at Henllys. Retired, and respectable farmer, David Owen lived here with his wife in what were described at the time as 'comfortable circumstances'. The couple employed domestic staff and had no money worries but Mr Owen became convinced that he was in decline, physically, socially and financially and 'would be better off in the workhouse'. On the morning of Wednesday, 4 January, Eluned, the maid, served Mr Owen his breakfast, as usual. He then went out and as he hadn't returned for lunch, Eluned went to look for him. Finding him in the coach-house she sought the assistance of neighbour Richard Roberts of Bodidda. Richard explained that having been called to Henllys coach-house he found David Owen, 'lying in a pool of blood, face downwards. His two sticks were in his hand, and on the ground

near him was an open razor'. The Coroner's verdict was, 'Suicide in a fit of depression'.

Retrace your steps as far as the council houses, where you turn right, descend the green and continue down the road. Cross Pont Gyffredin, turning left at the junction and continuing to Cyffredin, where you ascend the footpath opposite through the kissing gate. Pause at the first wooden field gate on the left and glance down at the huge ruin (13), to the right of Cyffredin, before continuing past an attractive old cottage to soon reach the roadway, going through two kissing gates on your way.

13. This was a candle factory whose products were highly regarded by local lead miners. Being tallow candles, they tended to drip much less than wax alternatives. Owen Owen, the candlemaker here in the 1880s and 1890s used to collect skins from slaughterhouses in Conwy and Penmaenmawr and deposit them at his depot behind the Harp Inn, Conwy, on the site of the old Woolworth's on High Street. When he had stripped off the fat he would employ his horse and cart to deliver it here for processing. Once inside the factory, the crude animal fat was chopped up, rendered down, clarified and poured into dipping troughs. Meanwhile the wicks were cut to the desired lengths, attached to a rod suspended over the trough and then the hanging wicks were dipped into the molten tallow before being removed and allowed to cool. This process was then repeated several times until the desired thickness of candle was reached.

Llywelyn Evans took over from Owen but gradually the decline in local mining, the increasing efficiency of oil lamps and the greater availability of electricity together conspired to reduce the demand for candles. The factory closed during the First World War.

Turn left, after 200 yards (180m) follow the footpath signs through 'Conwy Touring Park' past Bryn Hyfryd (14). Half way up the hill go through the kissing gate, next to the public footpath sign. Follow the footpath signs through two kissing gates. Cross the campsite lane, follow the track ahead. Ignore the first stile on your right, head for the stile in front of you. Head up the hill, keep going for 700 yards (640m), keeping with the right hand side of several fields. You will go through three kissing gates, before coming to a minor road.

14. In Victorian times Bryn Hyfryd was the home of William Hughes, the local postman. In the years between the growth of motorised transport and the widespread adoption of private transport, rural postmen helped keep open traditional rights of way. Before being supplied with vans postmen walked from farm to farm along these centuries-old footpaths whilst completing their daily deliveries.

15. Look carefully at the nameplate attached to the top of the metal gate, it reads 'Jabez Jones, maker of Hendre'; you visited his Victorian smithy at (10).

Turn right, after 200 yards (180m) cross the ladder stile on the left and follow the field path past Home Farm (16).

16. This is the Home Farm of the Benarth Estate, which established a legal monopoly over the whole one hundred and thirty-five acres that lie between you and Afon Conwy. At the heart of the estate and hidden from public view stands Benarth Hall, a magnificent Georgian country house of 1790, possibly the work of John Nash. The mansion was created for Samuel Price of Lincoln's Inn but sold by his executors in June 1805. The sale particulars described the house as: 'An elegant, commodious and modern built mansion house, suitable for a large family and with every description of offices'. It included 'beautiful pleasure grounds laid out with great taste and enriched with forest trees and the choicest evergreens', as well as a 'hot house, green house, pinery, melon pit, peachery and ice house'. The estate is still the preserve of wealthy owners and you are prohibited from walking down to the river, strolling through the pleasure grounds, or even allowing your gaze to alight upon that elegant and commodious mansion.

Continue over a series of ladder stiles and across fields for 800 yards (730m) before bearing left along the hedge, as indicated by a footpath arrow sign. Soon you enter the south-western fringe of Benarth Woods. Following the descending path, you soon emerge atop a steep bank with a panoramic view of Conwy ahead. Before descending to the road glance over at the second castle tower (17) from the railway bridge.

Afon Gyffin and Conwy castle

17. The contrasting stonework of the Bakehouse Tower and its buttress is evidence of extensive Victorian repair work. The rock on which the tower was constructed had disintegrated causing a huge section of the tower to collapse. Curiously, the top section remained intact but below that a yawning gap stretched almost the full length of the tower; the image was captured in a painting by Turner. As the railway runs along this southern flank of the castle, the London and North Western Railway Company agreed to stabilise and repair the tower at their own expense. The work was completed in April 1881.

Turn right along Llanrwst Road, passing the garage (18) on the left before crossing the bridge over the Gyffin stream (19) and turning left alongside the Guildhall to return along Rose Hill to Lancaster Square.

18. A century ago this was Peter and Humphrey Lewis' timber yard and steam saw mill. Humphrey was also a Conwy Councillor who lived at Muriau, which you pass, on your right, next to the former National School, as you return along Rose Hill.

19. Afon Gyffin formerly carried a much greater volume of water and was much wider at this point. The waters of Afon Gyffin lapped against the lower walls of the castle until the railway company altered its course to allow for the convenient laying of track and the creation of a goods yard (note the surviving railway crane). In the Middle Ages the Welsh were permitted to harbour their ships and receive supplies here, but they were not allowed to use the Conwy-town quay.

Originally published in
Walks from Conwy

by Christopher Draper

Carreg Gwalch Best Walks in the Conwy Valley

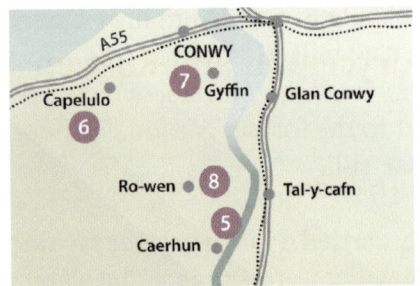

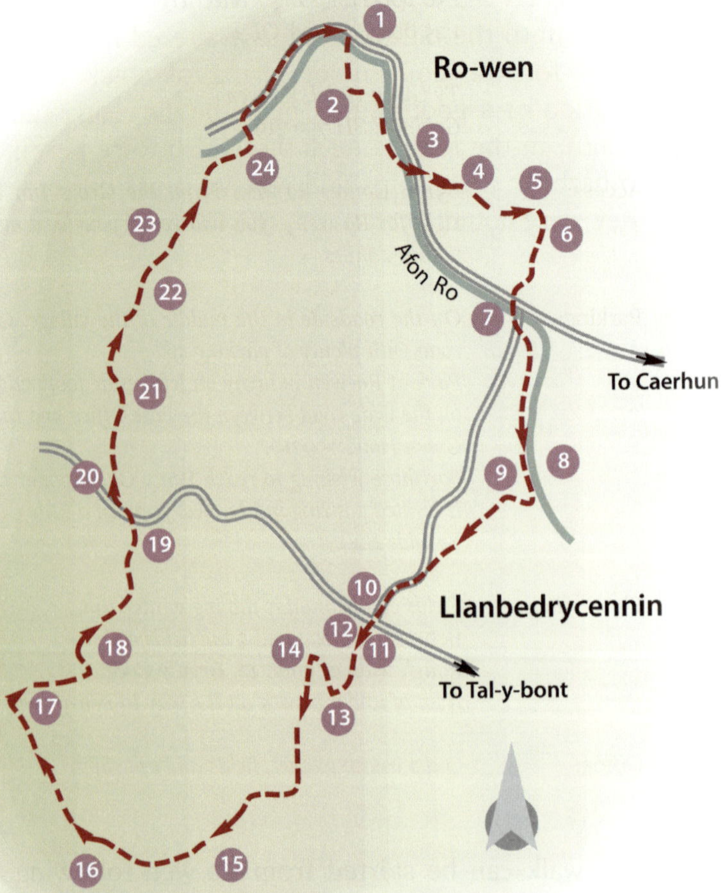

Walk 8
Around Llanbedrycennin and Ro-wen

Walk details
Approx distance: *7 miles/11.3 kilometres*

Approx time: *2½-3 hours*

O.S. Maps: *1:50 000 Landranger Sheet 115*
1:25 000 Explorer OL 17

Start: *Tŷ Gwyn Hotel, Ro-wen*
Grid Ref. SH 759 719

Access: *B5106 Conwy-Ro-wen. From the Groes Inn turn right for Ro-wen – you will reach your destination within 2 miles.*

Parking: *On the roadside in the middle of the village. Quiet road with plenty of parking spaces.*
Park at Ro-wen in layby on left beside footbridge or on the wide road between the Post Office and the Tŷ Gwyn Hotel 759719.
For those wishing to reach Pen y Gaer sooner there is limited parking in Llanbedrycennin a little east of Ye Olde Bull.

Please note: *Fields can be muddy during winter time.*
Between points 4 and 5 the fields are steep.
Rough walk at point 12, Bryn y Coed.
A lot of undergrowth on the way to Pen-y-gaer.

Going: *Quiet country lanes, fields and hill sides.*

The walk can be started from Ro-wen following the pleasant Afon Ro for a time, apart from a detour

Pen y Gaer from Bwlch y Ddeufaen

(optional) to climb a small hill for good views of the Conwy Valley. After going through the attractive village of Llanbedrycennin, with its simple medieval church, old tracks take you fairly gently up into the hills for a visit to Pen y Gaer. This Iron Age fort has 3 ramparts. Below its main entrance in the south west you will find many pointed stones set in the ground. These 'cheveux de frise' slowed enemy charges down so that defenders had more time to launch their missiles (arrows and stones). The return goes gently down the open hillside back to the quiet village of Ro-wen. There are good views of the valley in the higher sections of the walk, also the Carneddau range of mountains are seen from an unusual angle. Paths are usually

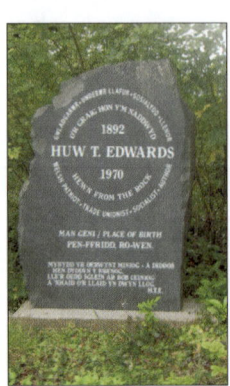

Memorial plaque at the start of the walk

mostly dry except at Point 14.

You can shorten the walk to 3¾ miles/6km at Point 19 by forking right at lane junction.

Walk directions

1. Cross footbridge and go on, soon between walls.

2. Just before gate, turn left along by hedge, then right to walk by river (on your left).

3. Unless you wish to stay on the road to Point 7, turn left over road and right down steps. Go on over field towards farmhouse to a gate just left of house.

Kissing gate at Point 3 of the walk

4. On along grass, left before white gate, then through right gate past sheds. On 15m then go left up field with wall on right and poles.

After farmhouse, path descends to left at Point 4 of the walk

The derelict farm at Pontwgan. The path goes between the farmhouse and the farm buildings, then out onto the road.

5. At field corner cross the low but rather awkward fence and go up field towards house. Then bear right to walk by iron fence. At hedge to left and at once right over stiles.

6. Go one third right to steps in hedge on crest of ridge. Go on down with hedge on your left. At next hedge go through the right-hand of 2 gaps and follow hedge (on your left) down to barn. Go on through gate just right of barn to road.

7. Go on across road, over bridge, and past houses to iron steps. Here go left to walk by Afon Ro.

After crossing over a stone bridge, look out for this iron stile on your right, which leads down to a river; Point 7 of the walk

Llanbedrycennin church

8. Just after bridge on left go over stile. Cross field keeping near farm on right.

9. Over stile near house and left to gate. Keep on with hedge on your right.

10. On along track, then road, past church to Ye Olde Bull.

11. Here fork right up lane and soon fork left.

12. At Bryn y Coed fork right up rough track. Go right through farm gate by pole and left along faint field path. Bear right by hedge (on your right) up to barns.

13. Here go left between barns and right along grass track passing just left of house

14. At next barns turn left up stony track. (If muddy go

Ye Olde Bull – a drovers' inn at Llanbedrycennin

through gate on right beside pens and follow faint path in bracken parallel to track.).

15. When wall on left ends follow wall on right to leat. Go on by leat.

16. Turn right over first bridge and on along track.

17. Go right up ladder stile over wall. The fort is reached after crossing wall at a second stile. Return to this stile but turn right along wall without crossing it.

18. Soon a wall stile is reached. Here turn two-thirds right down the left of two banks. Keep on when bank ends to reach gate into lane.

19. Down lane. Fork left at lane junction.

20. As lane bears left cross stile over wall and go north over field to pass just left of large pylon. Here a grassy

track leads to house. Use gate just right of house to reach road.

21. Turn left along road for 100m, then right between walls. Keep on over field with wall on your right. When wall bears right keep along clear path. When path becomes narrow make for ladder stile over wall about 100m ahead.

22. Over stile and on, soon beside sunken lane on right.

23. Over iron steps and down by fence and lane on right. Join track at gate.

24. Go over stile on right before house. Go down past sheep pens. Follow hedge for 50m and over stile on left. Go straight on past house on left to green gate, then straight on to road and right down it. Ignore turnings off to left.

Tŷ Gwyn inn, Ro-wen

Originally published in
Walks in North Snowdonia

by Don Hinson

Carreg Gwalch Best Walks in the Conwy Valley

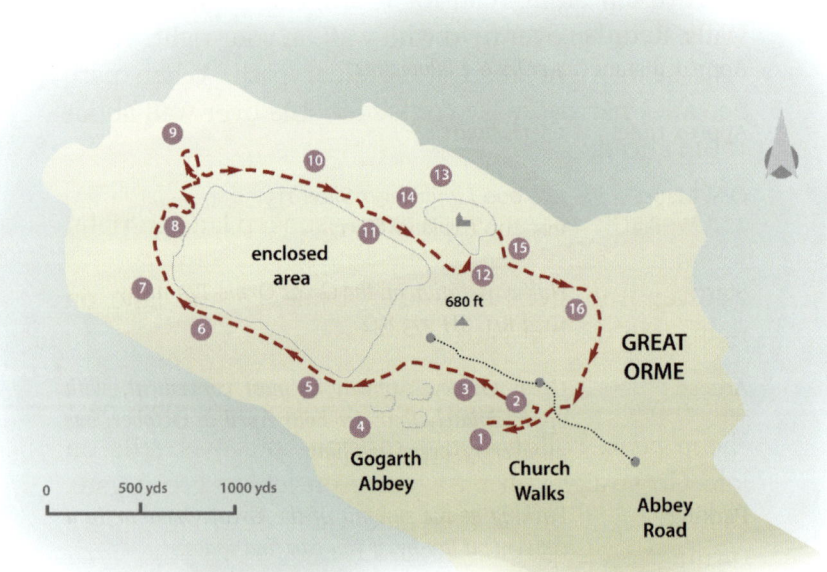

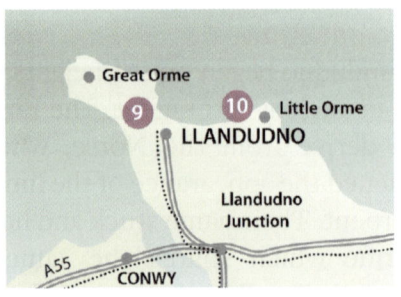

Walk 9
Ancient History on the Great Orme

Walk details
Approx distance: *4 miles/6.4 kilometres*

Approx time: *1½-1¾ hours*

O.S. Maps: *1:50 000 Landranger Sheet 115*
1:25 000 Explorer OL 17

Start: *Halfway station on the Great Orme Tramway Grid Ref. SH 773 832*

Access: *Great Orme Tramway is most convenient, with approximately four per hour April to October; bus number 73, every half hour.*

Parking: *Parking at the summit of the Great Orme or in a convenient lay-by, if you can find space.*

Please note: *Elevated but surprisingly level, well defined paths, dry surface in almost all weathers; but can be windy.*

Going: *Country lanes, country paths.*

Introduction
Llandudno began on the heights of the Great Orme. It is an ancient settlement. The English name is thought to derive from the Norse, when Viking marauders likened the appearance of the limestone headlands to a serpent. Their name stuck and has come down to us as Orme which shares the same derivation as 'The Worm's Head' in southern Wales. The Welsh name for the area is Gogarth, and both the Norse 'Orme' and

The prehistoric copper mine on the Great Orme

Welsh 'Gogarth' have existed together for many centuries. Yet the settlement on the Orme goes back much further than the Viking period. More than ten thousand years ago people were living in the caves dotted about the Orme. They used simple stone tools. By about 3000 BC they were making pots and cultivating the land. By 1500 BC they were digging out copper to combine with other minerals to produce a new wonder material; the Bronze Age had arrived in Llandudno. This walk illustrates these ancient times, and shows a little of subsequent developments.

The Walk and Points of Interest
After leaving the tram, walk back a little down Tŷ Gwyn Road, go through the gate next to the cattle grid and turn into St Beuno's Road on the right. After one hundred yards or so, turn into Cromlech Road, and go over the stile to view the cromlech (1).

1. This cromlech is called Llety'r Filiast whilst this part of the Orme is referred to as Maes y Facrell possibly because it is a sheltered spot that was used for drying the catch in the sun to preserve it. About 5,000 years ago this cromlech was built as a burial chamber by Neolithic people. It would originally have been covered with a shell of soil and turf, and may have served a dual purpose of also staking the group's right to use the surrounding area of territory. It has sustained considerable damage over the years, but remains a powerful image of life and death in the New Stone Age.

Retrace your steps back up Cromlech and St Beuno's Roads until you reach the junction, on the left, with Pyllau Road. Just ahead of you, on the right, are the buildings of the Bronze Age Copper Mine Centre (2).

2. A tour of these workings is highly recommended, because unlike many 'visitor attractions' this provides an intelligent experience with a resident archaeologist who will answer your most searching queries. There is an admission charge (tel. 01492-870447) but you can visit the bookshop and café (our later refreshment stop) without charge.

This Bronze Age Copper Mine is a heritage site of world importance. The oldest workings contained stone hammers, bone tools and charcoal which was carbon dated to about 1200 BC. A complex network of galleries has been discovered over an area of six acres, and extending to a depth of over 250 feet. The Bronze Age miners used stone hammers to bash out the ore from the softer, easier to work, rocks. The hammers themselves were selected from hard, rounded volcanic rocks they found on local beaches. When harder seams had to be penetrated, firesetting techniques were used. In easily worked areas simple tools of bone or antler were also used. Some of the galleries are very small, and suggest that children may well have helped mine for copper. These mines may have been abandoned when iron took over from bronze as the cutting edge material. It seems they may have been left unworked until they were reopened in the 17th century. In 1991 they were finally opened to the public.

Keep to the path on the left of the road, notice the quarried area (3) to your left.

3. The fossil quarry contains the remains of the oldest inhabitants of the Orme. Here are the shells of the creatures which lived in shallow seas 300 million years ago. The Bishop's Quarry alludes to its ownership by the Bishop of Bangor, who was granted the manor of Gogarth by Edward I soon after his success in the war of 1277. As Lord of the Manor, Bishop Anian had a substantial palace built for himself below you, nearer the shoreline on a lower level of the Orme. (It is now in ruins, and on the private land of the Old Abbey Residential Home.)

When you see an area ahead that has been fenced off to protect the heathland, turn left along the edge of the fence and continue until you notice a series of shallow pits (4) on your left.

4. These pits held vertical Brammock rods. These were hinged so as to transmit movement horizontally, from a water powered engine below you on the shoreline, to a mine pump situated 1,300 yards further up the slope.

This arrangement didn't prove very effective and was replaced by a more efficient steam engine powered pumping system.

Following the path round to the right, notice a dried-up spring (5). Keep the stone wall on your right.

5. Ffynnon Gogarth provided the water to power the 'Tom and Jerry' (named after characters in a book published in 1821) engine, which operated the Brammock rods.

Continuing ahead, notice a descending path (6) on your left (The Monks' Path).

6. The Monks' Path connected the Bishop's palace with St Tudno's church on the other side of the Orme. As Lord of the Manor of Gogarth his tenants would have had to fulfil certain duties, such as labour service and grinding corn at the Lord's mill, as well as paying an annual cash rent. There is therefore no doubt that this has long been an important path. Traditionally it was known as Ffordd Las, and 'The Monks' Path' name seems to have been a Victorian romanticization, loosely based on fact, but mainly devised to promote the areas charms for tourist purposes. The story goes that the path will miraculously remain green throughout the course of the longest drought because it was blessed by the passage of so many Holy Monks through the ages.

Do not descend The Monks' Path, but continue to follow your original route which continues around the outside of the old stone wall. The views are wonderful and this section is particularly peaceful. Soon, you reach a pile of stones (7) to your left.

7. This is thought to be a Bronze Age cairn or communal burial place, although passing walkers have undoubtedly added to the pile of stones.

Continue around the headland but stay at the same elevation. Before you turn to the east, notice a pit (8) about eighty yards from the wall.

8. This sink hole is an entirely natural phenomenon caused by the action of water on soluble limestone. The surrounding area is a limestone pavement with characteristic 'cracks' or grykes, which provide a sheltering environment for small plants.

Notice a standing stone (9) about two hundred yards to the north.

9. The exact role of this standing stone has not been clearly identified though, over the years, many have argued for an astronomical or mystical significance.

Follow the path until you notice a huge, distinctly unusual rock (10) off to the left.

10. The distinctive shape of this rock has been likened to that of the traditional 'cottage loaf'. When life in Llandudno was centred on the Orme, it was common practice for deals to be sealed by striking this rock. This explains its local name of, 'The Free Trade Loaf'. Like most of the huge, detached blocks of stone around you (and unlike the standing stone at [I]) this

arrived here through nature, and not by design. It is an example of a glacial erratic, a boulder carried along like a pebble in a stream, by the huge and powerful glaciers of the Ice Age. As the climate improved, the ice melted, and the boulders were left high and dry.

Continue, and soon you notice a water source (11) set into the wall on your right.

11. This is the Roman Well. Nearly two thousand years ago, the Romans forced their slaves to dig the ore from these mines and wash away the impurities here in these waters. Except that the stonework seems much more recent, and there is no evidence of Roman mining anywhere on the Great Orme! The masonry is most likely Victorian, and so is the story. The Victorians were adept at devising tall stories for gullible tourists like The Monks' Path or Gelert's Faithful Hound, or the ludicrous re-naming of Llanfair Pwllgwyngyll.

If you look down on the slopes below you, and also to the area above the churchyard, you will notice ridges in the turf (12).

12. These ridges are the remains of medieval farming. The use of oxen and heavy wooden ploughs left behind characteristic furrows. As arable farming was increasingly confined to lower levels, these slopes were given over to grazing, and where they were not obliterated by subsequent mine works the evidence persists. The use of aerial photography has greatly

facilitated the expert interpretation of such evidence in recent years.

Walk down to examine Saint Tudno's church (13) and its burial grounds (14).

13. Tudno was a 6th century Celtic missionary and it is interesting to note that Celtic churches were often named after their founders, whereas those of the Roman Church were usually dedicated to well-known saints or martyrs. Tudno probably built himself a simple wattle and daub shelter (or possibly even made do with a cave), whilst he set about establishing a church here on the Orme. His original church building would probably have been of wood, cut down from the trees that were then much more numerous on the Orme. In the 12th century a stone church was built, which was then enlarged in the 15th century. This building had its roof ripped off in a gale in 1839. The old church was abandoned and the new St George's church, further down in the newly-developing town, was consecrated in 1840 as the new parish church. Fortunately St Tudno's was re-roofed and restored in 1855, and in the summer, it still continues its long tradition of open air services.

14. In the new cemetery, surmounted by an astonishing (and easy to spot) white old-style winged motor racing wheel, is the grave of Beatrice Blore Browne, 1887-1921, with the brief epitaph, 'She Feared Naught But God'. Beatrice and her husband pioneered motoring in northern Wales. In 1911 they organised a successful publicity stunt which involved driving four Darracq cars up to the summit of the Great Orme. Nearby lies

the simpler headstone of a family; 'Who Lost Their Lives in the Dolgarrog Disaster of November 2nd 1925', when a dam burst and swept away much of the original Conwy Valley village. Up in the corner, away from the sea and slightly overgrown, is a splendid monument in relief of a Victorian hiker, with the epitaph: 'Erected with sincere affection and esteem to William Smith by the Llandudno mountaineering club and friends. In remembrance of many hours of good fellowship, 1899'.

Near to the church in the old graveyard there are five more gravestones of particular historical interest. Alice Tarrey lost her life on the wooden paddle steamer, the *Rothsay Castle*, which began to take in water off the Orme whilst on a voyage in bad weather from Liverpool to the Menai Strait. She sank on 17 August, 1831 drowning Alice and one hundred and eight other passengers. The son of John Bright, the well-known Victorian statesman has a simple white headstone announcing that he died 'aged nearly six, November 8th, 1864'. Jonathan Rawlings died 1836; George Edwards died 1813; and William James died 1827; were all agents for copper mines on the Orme. Each has a horizontal slate headstone which provide further details of their lives.

Leave the churchyard by the gate to the south-east, cross the road, and follow the marked path until you soon notice a spring on your right (15).

15. Ffynnon Powell is named after the family that brought it into being! Distressed by the persistence of a

On the Great Orme

summer drought they retired to St Tudno's to implore God's help. After a serious session of prayer they began to return home along this track when, lo and behold, they realised that God had indeed responded. Bubbling up from the ground was the never-failing water supply you see before you.

Continue along the track until you reach an old farm (16).

16. This is Penymynydd Isaf which is also called the Pink Farm; away to the right you should also be able to see Penymynydd Ucha, which is sometimes called the White Farm. Both farmhouses are substantially 18th century dwellings, although farming has been carried on here for much longer. Both farms quickly realised that there was money to be made from the influx of Victorian ramblers on the Orme and both operated as refreshment rooms. This became 'The Farm Inn', which had a full drinks licence, but alas no more.

Follow the lane on the right, and soon you should be able to recognise the starting point of our walk, from the halfway station you can return to the town by tram; but it is recommended to first continue across to the Copper Mines complex (2) for refreshments and underground explorations.

2. Copper Mines Tea Room
Address: Pyllau Road, Great Orme, Llandudno, tel. 01492-870447

Refreshments: Tea, coffee, soft drinks, sandwiches, cakes, baked potatoes and cooked meals.

Description: Although part of the Great Orme Bronze Age Copper Mine complex the cafe building itself has no great history but it is attractively decorated, quiet and the food is good. You can eat here and visit the bookshop even if you choose not to take the tour of the mine workings.

Originally published in
Walks from Llandudno

by Christopher Draper

Carreg Gwalch Best Walks in the Conwy Valley

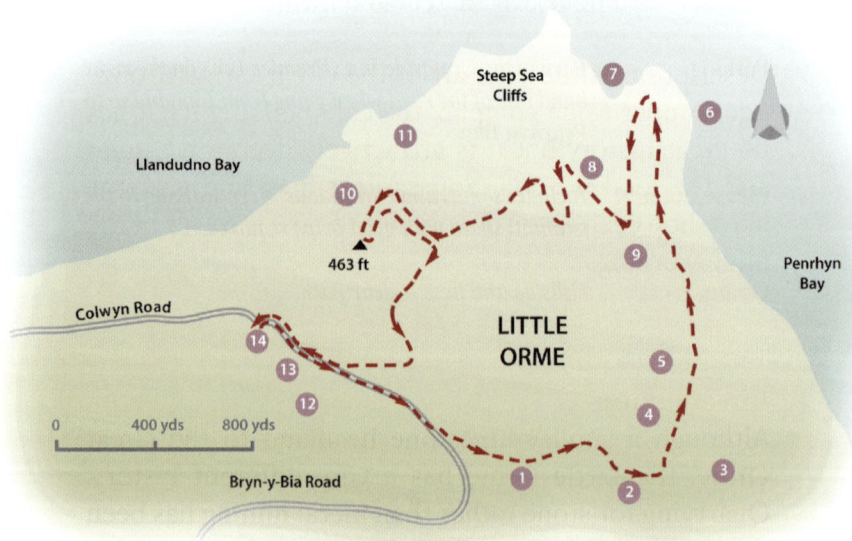

Walk 10
Exploring the Little Orme

Walk details
Approx distance: *2½ miles/4 kilometres*

Approx time: *1½-2 hours*

O.S. Maps: *1:50 000 Landranger Sheet 116*
1:25 000 Explorer OL 17

Start: *Foot of Penrhynside Hill, Little Orme, Llandudno Grid Ref. SH 814 821*

Access: *Bus 12, 13, 14, 15 or 16 at fifteen minute intervals.*

Parking: *Park in the Craigside Inn (Premier Inn) on the right hand side of the road when going from Llandudno to Penrhyn Bay.*

Please note: *Includes some rather strenuous, steep walking to the summit; shoes with good grips required.*

Going: *Hillside and lane – clear path.*

Introduction
Although a similar limestone headland to the Great Orme, the Little Orme has a very different history. Quarrying for stone rather than metal mining has been the most significant activity here, and this quarrying was only developed commercially some thirty years after mining ceased on Y Gogarth. Although much smaller in size than the Great Orme, many consider the view from the top to be superior. On our route to the summit we will also visit the little cove of Porth

Two views of the scenery on the Little Orme

Dyniewaid, one of the most secluded spots in Creuddyn. In the words of an 1892 guidebook:

> On trip days when the Happy Valley and the Telegraph Station are in full swing . . . a stroll over this comparatively neglected height will specially commend itself to the less exuberant class of visitors.

The Walk and Points of Interest

Walk uphill and cross to the Tŷ Ucha farm lane, marked by a footpath sign. Walk along to the farm and ignore the arrow to the left; your right of

way is ahead, between the house and the outbuildings (1).

1. This is Tŷ Ucha, the only remaining farm on the Little Orme. The style of the house suggests that it may have been substantially modernised about 1876 when a new tenant insisted in his lease that necessary repairs be carried out by the Mostyn Estate. The outbuildings have been altered less, and appear to be about two hundred years old. The old stone barn cleverly takes advantage of the sloping ground, with a single-storey cowshed at one end and a cartshed with hayloft over at the other. As you pass through the buildings notice, on the left, the old stone pigsties with typical metal gates.

Go through the gate and continue along the footpath following the footpath signs which was, until the mid-19th century, the main approach to the farm. Turn left after going through the kissing gate. Soon you emerge onto a wider lane, with two old dwellings ahead, both created from Pentre Isa farmstead (2).

2. Pentre Isa farmhouse was built in 1680 but lost much of its character with its conversion into two separate dwellings in the 1970s. If the plans to develop Llandudno as the main ferry port for Ireland, instead of Holyhead, had succeeded, than Pentre Isa would have suffered an earlier and even more severe loss of character. The plan was to take the railway across Pentre Isa land, and through the Little Orme in a tunnel starting near where you are now standing. The dwelling opposite was converted from one of Pentre Isa's barns.

Continue, passing between the two dwellings. Go through the kissing gate and glance over to the right at Penrhyn Beach Estate (3).

3. The modern Penrhyn Beach Estate was developed in the 1970s, largely from the farm land of Pentre Isa.

Continue ahead, and notice the extensive remains of quarrying (4) all around.

4. This is largely the result of the activities of The Little Orme's Head Limestone Company. Their 1889 lease gave quarrying rights over about forty acres of the Little Orme, and by the turn of the century they were employing about eighty people here. The main business was to extract and ship the limestone to the Clyde and Argyll coast ports for use in blast furnaces and the chemical industries. Over the years, the ownership of the company changed and the nature of the quarrying shifted towards extracting and crushing the stone as an ingredient of Portland Cement.

Continue, passing to the right of the huge quarry basin (5).

5. After the war new ideas for the commercial exploitation of the Little Orme were produced. In 1952 it was proposed to create a caravan site here with this basin being filled with water and used as a boating lake. In 1974 the site was proposed as a tip with the basin being filled with rubbish. In 1981 the plan was to fill the basin with the excavations from the new A55 expressway that was then being constructed. Local opposition scuppered all of these schemes.

As you pass the end of the basin, wonderful sea vistas open up before you; but do notice the still impressive remains of the old stone quays (6) down to the right.

6. In the early years of the quarry, wooden wagons were hauled up and down an incline to the wharf below; but in the early years of the new century this system was replaced with concrete hoppers sited above the wharves, and disgorging directly into ships. The stone simply slid into the hoppers along metal troughs, from the crushing plant above. One thousand ton capacity ships could berth here and be filled in less than an hour.

Walk on towards the headland until you can see a little rocky cove (7) far below on the left.

7. The cove is Porth Dyniewaid, and the rocky headland is Trwyn y Fuwch. Notice that the quarry works were effectively screened from Llandudno by this headland. The freehold owners, Mostyn Estates, wanted to maximise their income from their quarry leases here, but they did not want an unsightly quarry to reduce the rental value of their Llandudno properties by spoiling their vistas. The Mostyns therefore included restrictive covenants in their leases which precluded quarrying on the Llandudno side. It was even prohibited to allow smoke to be visible from Llandudno.

This is a wonderful spot, peaceful yet dramatic. It is possible to climb down to the shore here, with care. Turn around and run your eyes along the heights over on your right – can you spot a long grassy slope or incline? This is where we are heading. Make your way over to it and

carefully ascend to the top, go through the kissing gate, where you will see a metal winding wheel (8).

8. The incline you just walked up was the track bed for the trucks whose ascent and decline was controlled by steel cables from the winding wheel. Stone was extracted from the faces you can see; it then descended via the incline to the processing and crushing works, and then along the shutes to the hoppers, awaiting shipping. This is a good vantage point for spotting the extensive track beds on the lower levels, especially when there are good shadows. You should be able to make out the marks left by the old railway sleepers. The quarry operated its own three-foot gauge railway with four steam locomotives. During the First World War these were driven by women, who also operated the compressed air rock drills and loaded and unloaded the wagons. Although the company were still managing to extract about a quarter of a million tons of stone a year, they ceased all production here at the end of 1931. Many of their buildings remained for some time, with the concrete hoppers only being demolished in 1987.

Our route now turns to the left, but do glance down at the extensive level area below. It had another brief life after the quarrying ended when it was taken over by the military (9).

9. In 1917 it was suggested that this site might make a good prisoner-of-war camp, but the authorities didn't take up the suggestion. In 1941, just ten years after serious quarrying had ended, the War Department

requisitioned the site as a practice camp for coastal artillery. The redundant quarry buildings were used, along with a newly-erected assortment of Nissen huts and giant guns. Firing would take place night and day, much to the excitement of local children and the irritation of their parents. As the war drew to a close, the camp was run down and its functions and equipment moved elsewhere. You can still find the concrete bases and metal stanchions left behind, but it is not easy to distinguish these from the remains of the quarry works.

Continue upwards following the yellow footpath arrows until you reach a point where a path goes off to the right, following a sort of shallow valley between two peaks, (remember this point, because we shall be returning!). Take this path, and then turn to the left when you see a wooden post ahead. Keep ascending until you reach the triangulation post (10) which soon comes into view.

10. You are now standing at a height of 463 feet. Although it is 200 feet lower than the Great Orme, many consider the view from here to be much finer. There are few obstructions to your view because the grassy slopes drop away so sharply. Perhaps the conspirators who, in 1580, gathered in a cave just 100 feet or so further down these slopes thought that such hazards would ensure their safety. Danger for Father William Davies existed in the shape of the newly-established church, for he was a Catholic priest using the cave to print traitorous Popish tracts. This was the first printing press in Wales. The authorities discovered the cave, probably through an informer, and William Davies was apprehended and sentenced to

death. He was informed that the death sentence would be quashed if he renounced Catholicism. He refused and was hung, drawn and quartered at Beaumaris. This cave is located at OS 813 825 but you should not attempt to find it as the slope is far too hazardous.

Before you leave this marvellous viewpoint, perhaps another story might serve to illustrate the notoriously dangerous sea cliffs (11) here.

11. In the year 1900 there was a chap working at Pentre Isa farm called William Edwards. William was twenty-five and planning to marry Mary Davies who worked at Tŷ Ucha farm in Llandudno. Everyone knew that visitors to Llandudno were prepared to pay a shilling each for birds' eggs, and the money would come in handy for the forthcoming wedding. On Saturday evening, 5 May, Mary had been out with William and they parted at nine o'clock the best of friends, promising to meet the next day at Llangystennin at six o'clock. On Sunday morning William set out from Pentre Isa to do some egg collecting. He never arrived for his assignation with Mary. William's body was found wedged between boulders at the foot of the cliffs by a Police Constable Richards. The Constable said it appeared that William had fallen from the top of the Little Orme.

If you walk about twenty paces due south (use map as reference) of the trig. point you should be able to see two small stone houses (12) below you. They have patterned roofs made up of contrasting coloured slates.

12. The land and buildings on the far side of the high limestone wall were all part of the Shimdda Hir Estate.

On the Little Orme

We will presently visit the main house for our refreshments, but first notice the two moderate-sized stone houses on the brow of the hill. These were built in about 1880 as staff residences, one for the gardener and the other for the coachman. No longer connected to the big house they are now private residences.

Retrace your steps to the point of return (do you remember?). This time, take the path to the right; it may seem a little hidden by the gorse but it is actually part of the official North Wales Path as the waymarked arrows indicate. Go through the wooden kissing gate, following the path, with the information board on your right. This is a delightful section which curves as it descends around the hill, finally emerging at the main road through a wooden kissing gate. Cross with care, turn right and continue until you reach our refreshment place (13).

An old quarry on the Little Orme

13. This driveway serves what was originally the stable block to Shimdda Hir. Like the staff cottages you noticed earlier, it was erected around 1880 when the old Shimdda Hir farmstead was given a complete makeover to replace its agricultural appearance with the character of a 'Gentleman's Residence'. In 1968, along with the main residence it was bought by the Carmelite Religious Order and became St Mary's Convent. The nuns left in 1984 and the stables and main house subsequently passed into separate ownership, with the stables undergoing conversion to a private residence. In 1907, 452 bronze coins of the Roman period were discovered opposite here, on the other side of the road. Workmen were excavating rubble for road building near the Grand Theatre in Llandudno. By the time someone noticed the coins, they'd already transported some of the rubble. When they had a sift through the roadworks they found over a hundred more coins, so keep your eyes open . . .

12. Craigside Inn

Address: Colwyn Road, Llandudno (tel. 01492-545943)

Refreshments: Good range of bar and restaurant meals with the addition of options designed for children.

Description: The Craigside Inn was originally the big house of the Shimdda Hir Estate. It has been extended and modernised over the years, but the original farmhouse was probably erected in the 18th century. Over the years the estate land has varied from ten to thirty acres but now the associated cottages, land and stables have all passed into separate ownership. Whitbread Plc purchased this, the main residence, in the late 1980s. They have created an attractive, comfortable inn with an excellent range of play facilities for children.

Originally published in
Walks from Llandudno

by Christopher Draper

Carreg Gwalch Best Walks in the Conwy Valley

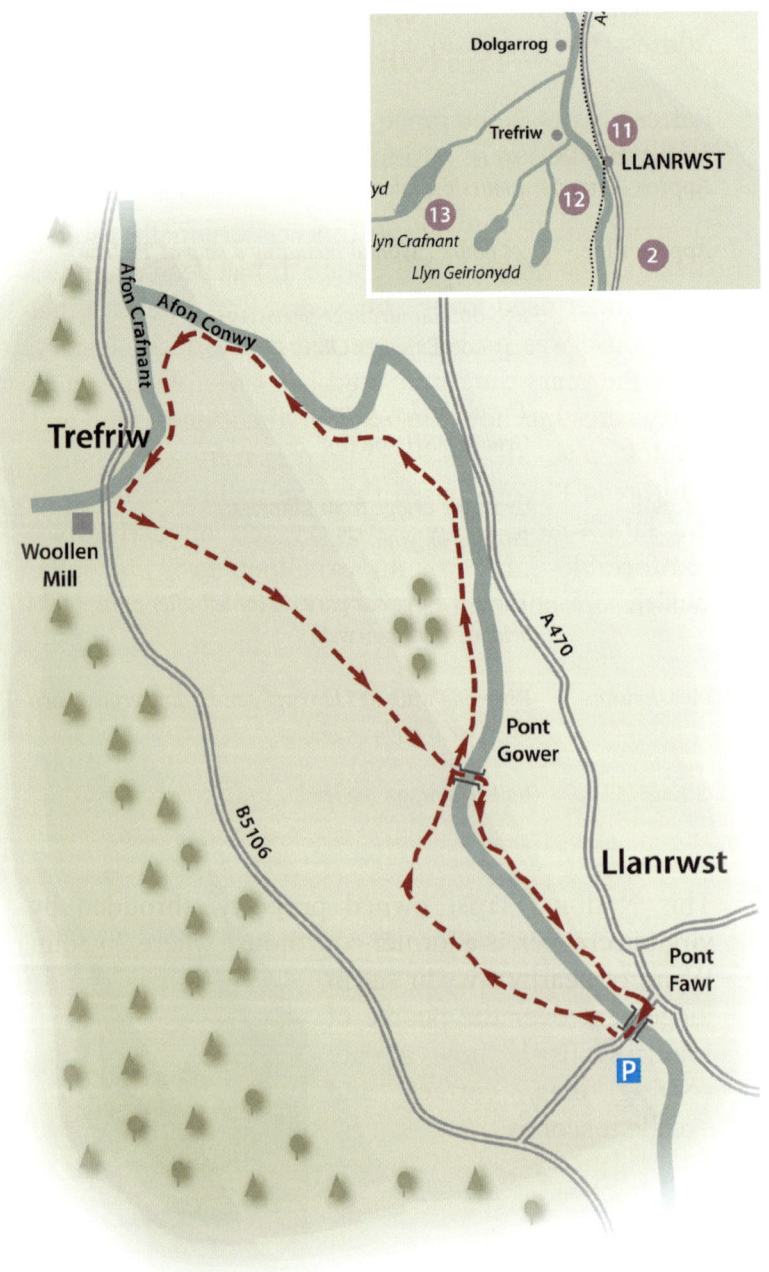

Walk 11
Tu Hwnt i'r Bont

Walk details

Approx distance:	*4 miles/6.4 kilometres*
Approx time:	*1¾ hours (without including a stop at Trefriw)*
O.S. Maps:	*1:50 000 Landranger Sheet 115* *1:25 000 Explorer OL 17*
Start:	*The old bridge, Llanrwst* *Grid Ref. SH 798 615*
Access:	*Cross the bridge from Llanrwst.* *Parking on your left.*
Parking:	*There is a free car park on the left after crossing the bridge from Llanrwst.*
Please note:	*Riverside walk at Llanrwst can be dangerous when the river is high.*
Going:	*Valley floor, on the level.*

This National Trust owned property, shrouded by virginia creeper, is a former courthouse where Sir John Wynn of nearby Gwydir sat in judgement over the people of Llanrwst. It is now a cafe serving teas, coffees and excellent scones.

The walk – from the old bridge at Llanrwst to Tu Hwnt i'r

Bont and then following the path along Afon Conwy to Trefriw and back to Llanrwst.

Start near the old bridge at Llanrwst – Pont Fawr. Cross the road towards Tu Hwnt i'r Bont, and then look for a Public Footpath sign on the right. Go down the track and after ½ km you will see a stile on your right just after a sharp bend to the left. Go over it and follow the path that runs along a ditch in the right-hand side of the field. Go over another stile and continue in the same direction past a small lake to another stile. Go over it and straight ahead over a small bridge and over a stile. You will then go over another stile and walk along the embankment that runs parallel to Afon Conwy.

Go to your right over the stile and continue along the embankment towards a bridge. An information board near the bridge explains recent steps taken to reduce flood risk in this area. Don't go over the footbridge (Pont Gower) nor to the left but go straight ahead over the two stiles and along the embankment. Go through the kissing gate and continue along the embankment and through another kissing gate near some pools. Continue along the embankment, through two kissing gates and then the path goes to the left away from the river.

Looking back from Pont Gower

Go through the kissing gate and continue along the embankment, then turn left and rejoin the river. Go through two kissing gates and continue along the embankment before turning left towards Trefriw. Follow the embankment that now runs parallel to Afon Crafnant, through two kissing gates, but don't go over the bridge on your right. Go through the kissing gate to a track and a public footpath sign. Go through the gate and along the path that runs between two fences. Go through a gate, pass a public toilet on your left and go out into the main road at Trefriw. In front of you is the woollen mill. Why not spend some time in Trefriw? There are two pubs here, a cafe, shops and the chalybeate wells.

Turn left and follow the narrow road that goes past a caravan park (not the main road). At the end of the road, follow the path passing a flood lake on your right, over the new embankment, between the playing field and the recreation ground. You will then reach a lane; follow it for 1 km to the footbridge. Go over this and turn right, over the stile to the riverside path. Go over two stiles, keeping on the riverside path, until you come to the decking. Follow the decking causeway over the bridge, continuing on the slate path, passing St Grwst's church and then up the steps to the street. Turn right and go over the bridge back to the car park.

Looking back from Pont Gower

Tu Hwnt i'r Bont, Llanrwst

Other Points of Interest

Afon Conwy The river rises from Llyn Conwy near Penmachno in Snowdonia and over its 36-mile length drops nearly 1,500 feet before it reaches the coast near Conwy. Its short length makes its level rise and fall very quickly when it rains heavily in the mountains. The river is tidal up to Llanrwst (about 14 miles from the sea) and at one time small ships and boats used to sail as far as here. At the turn of the 20th century pleasure boats came up the river to Trefriw bringing trippers – up to a thousand a day – from Conwy, Llandudno and Deganwy, for fishing, climbing, painting and in the recreation ground golf, tennis, bowls, croquet and quoits. The chalybeate wells have attracted visitors here from the 1800s to take the sulphur-iron rich waters. The wells date back to the Roman period when the Twentieth Legion had its headquarters in Caerhun lower down the valley.

Pont Gower

During the 19th century the pump room and baths were developed as a curative centre. Trefriw's heyday as a tourist resort ended during the Second World War due to silting of the river, but visitors still come here by car and bus to visit the spa baths and woollen mill.

Embankment The cob was built around 1815 although there have been numerous extensions and improvements since then. The valley was prone to flooding a number of times a year and the ground tended to be waterlogged and difficult to farm. At the beginning of the 19th century, the Reverend Walter Davies described the land as '... a perfect bog, partly peat, partly clay, producing a scanty crop of short and sour hay.' The main landowner, the Earl of Ancaster, embarked on a scheme to improve the farmland by digging drainage ditches and enclosing the land with the embankment. Despite the defences, the Conwy

Pont Fawr, Llanrwst

broke through the embankment and flooded the area twice in 2004, after very heavy rain.

Pont Gower The original bridge was a timber trestle construction built in the 19th century to link Trefriw with the railway station in Llanrwst, from where visitors would be taken by horse-drawn carriage to the Trefriw health spa. Some of the timber foundations of the original bridge are still visible underneath the modern suspension bridge.

Pont Fawr It is believed to have been designed by Inigo Jones and was built in 1636. This graceful triple-arched structure served the ancient counties of Caernarfonshire and Denbighshire as the only valley crossing until the construction of Thomas Telford's iron bridge at Betws-y-coed and suspension bridge at Conwy in the 19th century. Pont Fawr Llanrwst was a vital component in the defence of northern Wales during the English Civil War and in the latter half of the conflict Royalist troops blew up the western arch of the bridge to halt the advance of Parliamentarian artillery.

Llanrwst – is a town shrouded in myth, legend and a history dating back 1,500 years and having altered very little in the last 400 years. By the 10th century there was a sizeable settlement on this site, which in AD 954 saw the brutal and bloody Battle of Llanrwst, a decisive battle between the forces of northern and southern Wales. The town was wasted by an English army in 1403 because of its staunch support of Owain Glyndŵr's revolution and it suffered once again during the Wars of the Roses, when it was completely destroyed by Yorkist troops under the leadership of William Herbert, Earl of Pembroke. The town is proud of its independent roots and found itself in the No Man's Land of past wars. It still bears the motto: *'Cymru, Lloegr a Llanrwst'* (Wales, England and Llanrwst). Llanrwst Almshouses were constructed in 1610 by Sir John Wynn of Gwydir to house twelve poor men of the parish. They continued to provide shelter until 1976 when the buildings closed. Then in 1996 with the aid of Heritage Lottery funding they were restored and in 2002 opened as a museum of local history and a community focal point. It consists of two restored period rooms, temporary exhibitions and local artefacts. A working herb garden is situated in the museum grounds. Sadly the museum is closed at present

St Grwst's church It is dedicated to the Celtic saint Grwst, a 6th century Welsh missionary who settled in

St Grwst church, Llanrwst

Dyffryn Conwy. The present church, although constructed in 1170, dates from 1470, rebuilt two years after its destruction by Yorkist troops. The church houses a beautiful rood screen, a relic of the Cistercian Abbey at Maenan, built in 1509. The Wynn side-chapel was built in 1634 as a family mausoleum and houses rare examples of Stuart-period memorials. The chapel is home to the stone sarcophagus of Llywelyn ap Iorwerth, known as Llywelyn Fawr, and the effigy of Hywel Coetmor, a local knight who fought under the Black Prince at Poitiers and returned home to participate in the Glyndŵr Rebellion. Both structures are Grade I listed buildings. Open for accompanied viewing are a reproduction of a fresco depicting the Last Supper (from the Santa Maria Monastery in Milan), the ancient Llanrwst Bell and the spur of Dafydd ap Siencyn, the local 15th century outlaw. The church has recently undergone a programme of restoration funded by the Heritage Lottery Fund.

The woollen mill at Trefriw

Trefriw At one time Trefriw was an important trading centre and was regarded as the biggest inland port in Wales. Merchandise was brought up river from the coast and boats returned with slate, ore and timber from the surrounding hills. It was also an important wool-manufacturing centre. The mill was established before the industrial revolution, with its fulling mill taking already woven cloth from the cottages to wash and finish.

Originally published in
National Trust Walks 1. Northern Wales

by Dafydd Meirion

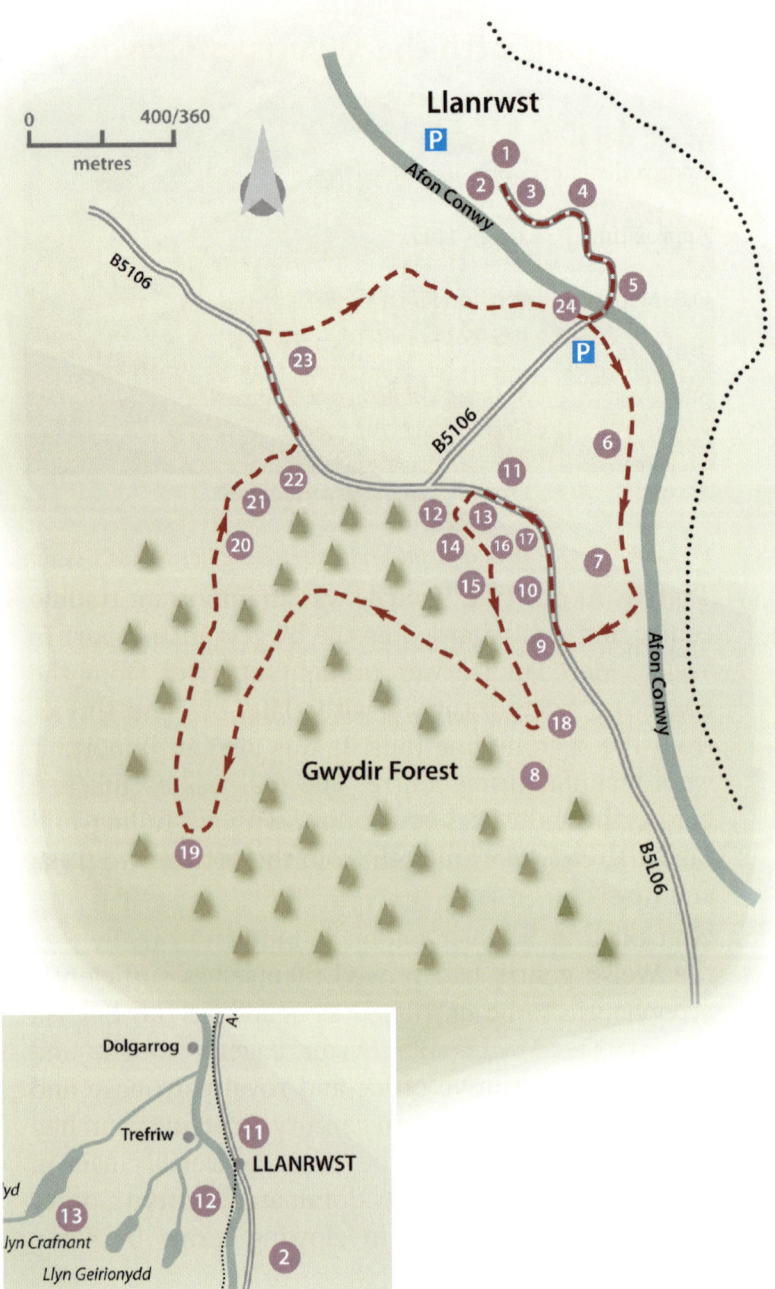

Walk 12
Walking with the Wynns of Gwydir

Walk details
Approx distance: *4 miles/6.4 kilometres*

Approx time: *2¼-2½ hours*

O.S. Maps: *1:50 000 Landranger Sheet 115*
    1:25 000 Explorer OL 17

Start: *St Grwst's churchyard, Llanrwst*
    Grid Ref. SH 797 616

Access: *From the town square, Llanrwst.*

Parking: *Park over the bridge on your left or behind Glasdir centre in Station Road, Llanrwst.*

Please note: *Some forestry tracks and footpaths.*

Going: *Field paths and country lanes.*

Introduction
From the Statute of Rhuddlan of March 1284 until the Act of Union of February 1536 the Conwy Valley was controlled by English colonial administrators. By 1536 the Welsh gentry had proved themselves sufficiently sycophantic to be entrusted as agents of the English Crown. The Wynns of Gwydir eagerly sought and gained administrative office and royal patronage and before the close of the 16th century Sir John Wynn had established himself as the most powerful man in northern Wales. The family dominated Dyffryn Conwy and are still spoken of in glowing terms by some

Gwydir castle, Llanrwst

commentators, but as we walk in their footsteps around the places they knew well, we examine their reputation.

The Walk and Points of Interest

To reach Gwydir Chapel (1) from Ancaster Square (4) walk down the lane at the side of the Eagles Hotel, past the almshouses (3) and enter St Grwst's church (2). Continue through the main body of the church and turn right into the chapel.

1. Gwydir Chapel was erected in 1633-4 by Sir Richard Wynn and contains the remains of, and memorials to, many members of the family. In the east corner is a white marble setting out the elaborate pedigree of the family. Under the traditional Welsh political system clan and kindred were crucial. Loyalty and support were owed and given within enduring relationships of kinship rather than to a more abstract concept of the 'State'. Sir John Wynn (1553-1627) famously wrote a

book that purports to be a family history but was primarily intended to establish the Wynns as legitimate offspring of the Princes of Wales. The Wynns intended to exploit kin loyalty to enhance the family's value to the English establishment. Where the Welsh nobility had once rallied resistance to English domination, after the Act of Union the native gentry rushed to become more English than the English! The Wynns were particularly impatient to ingratiate themselves with the Crown. The Statutes of Union may have banned the use of the Welsh language from all official proceedings and documents, effectively making ordinary folk foreigners in their own land, but for the gentry it provided golden opportunities. The Welsh upper classes were enabled to become magistrates, merchants, courtiers or members of parliament. John Wynn ap Maredudd was the first of the family to scramble aboard the gravy train, becoming High Sheriff of Caernarfonshire in 1544-45, 1553-54 and 1556-57 and MP for the county from 1551 to 1553. He died on the 9 July, 1559 and is commemorated here by a small white marble tablet bearing a Latin inscription. His son, Maurice Wynn, was the first of the family to abandon traditional Welsh naming practice and adopt the English form of surname, as recommended to the Welsh by King Henry VIII. This was a powerful sign of where the family's new loyalties lay. The Wynns had abandoned the struggle for independence pursued by Llewelyn ap Iorwerth, whose stone coffin lies here an enduring reminder of more honourable times.

2. In the main body of the church is an exquisite oak rood screen separating the nave from the chancel. This

screen, composed of intricately carved birds, fish, foliage and weird dragons, was pillaged from Maenan Abbey by the Wynns following the dissolution of the monasteries. Besides this screen the squires of Gwydir 'acquired' tons of building materials and acres of land from the destruction of the monastery and its estates. However, when Sir John Wynn tried to also grab the tithe income of this church, Bishop William Morgan staunchly defended the rights of the rector. When Wynn, in 1604, turned the screws on him to hand over the cash Morgan wrote to a friend, 'I were better rob by the highway side than do that which he requesteth'. Morgan went on to describe Sir John Wynn as 'a sacrilegious robber of my church, a perfydiouse spoyler of my diocese and an unaturall hynderer of preachers and good scholers'.

3. These almshouses were erected between the winter of 1610 and spring of 1612 as part of the Jesus Hospital Foundation to accommodate twelve poor people, 'eleven men and one old woman for their bedmaker'. There are twelve single room dwellings, six on each floor, with those on the upper floor reached by stairs at the rear. The groundfloor apartment at the western end was made into a passageway in 1812 to give access to the warden's house, which was being remodeled. The almshouses were endowed by Sir John Wynn, who also endowed a grammar school in Llanrwst but didn't consider it good enough for his own sons who were variously educated at Eton, Westminster, Bedford, Lincoln's Inn and St John's College, Cambridge. Although these almshouses continued to shelter the needy for more than three centuries, they were consistently hampered by the determination of the

Gwydir household to improperly channel income from the almshouse endowment into their own capacious coffers.

4. According to Sir John Wynn before the rise of his family this square was run-down and deserted. His *History of the Gwydir Family* not only describes the scene, but identifies the culprit; 'for Owain Glyndŵr's wars . . . brought such a desolation that green grass grew on the market-place in Llanrwst called Bryn-y-boten and the deer fed in the churchyard of Llanrwst, as it is reported, for it was Owain Glyndŵr's policy to bring all things to waste, that the English should find not strength nor resting-place in the country'. This is spin-doctoring of a high order. Sir John's famous *History* is a masterpiece of self-justification. Having constructed a specious pedigree asserting the family's inbred superiority, the book seeks to illustrate the destructive folly of Welsh leaders who opposed domination by the English Crown. By implication, and in contrast, he suggests the collaborationist policy of the Wynns was delivering peace, prosperity and social advance. In reality the run-down state of Llanrwst owed more to the effects of the de-population caused by the plague than to Glyndŵr's scorched earth policy. The plague had also hastened the collapse of the old social order and created vacant landholdings, which were systematically appropriated by the Wynns.

After retracing your steps to Ancaster Square turn right down Bridge Street and continue over Pont Fawr (5). At the far end turn left and continue along the riverside path, passing through a kissing gate beside the football ground you soon catch sight of Gwydir Castle (6) behind the trees,

with its characteristic tall chimneys across to the right.

5. Pont Fawr was built in 1636 to replace a bridge that 'had fallen into the greatest decay'. The costs of £1,000 were raised jointly by the counties of Denbighshire and Caernarfonshire, which it connected. Its elegant design is often ascribed to Inigo Jones and although this is unproven, as Queen Henrietta Maria's Treasurer, Sir Richard Wynn was acquainted with the famous architect and may well have invited him to produce drawings for this project. When an enormous river pearl was discovered in laying foundations for the bridge the obsequious Sir Richard presented it to the queen who subsequently incorporated into the Crown Jewels.

6. The parkland of Gwydir Castle originally extended to the river. The oldest parts of the building date back to 1500, the time of Maredudd ap Ieuan ap Robert, Sir John Wynn's great grandfather, but Gwydir Castle now appears much as it did when Sir John took over in 1580.

Soon after passing a football ground on the right you notice some large blocks of stone along the river-bank and a wide flat topped wall (7) stretching across the fields to the right.

7. This raised, stone causeway, which encloses the southern flank of the castle gardens was constructed by Sir John Wynn in the 1590s and by the 19th century was referred to as the 'Chinese Walk'. Here at the badly-preserved eastern end was a quay built to receive supplies for Gwydir Castle. Sir John Wynn made Afon Conwy navigable as far as Gwydir for small ships and barges and surviving accounts show that he regularly received supplies of spices, fine wines and tobacco from London, via Beaumaris. The Chinese Walk is altogether some 550 yards (500m) long, 7 feet high (2m) and 5 feet (1.5m) wide and at the Gwydir end concludes with a flight of eight slatestone steps.

Continue along the riverbank for 660 yards (600m) and immediately after crossing a stile turn right. Notice the rocky crag (8) looming up ahead (and slightly to the left) and follow the fence across the field over the stile, to exit onto the old Betws-y-coed road over the stile. Note the derelict structure (9) across the road opposite (and a little to the left).

8. The forested crag up ahead, 'Carreg Gwalch', concealed 'Old Siencyn's Cave', the legendary home of Dafydd ap Siencyn, Dyffryn Conwy's own Robin Hood. Siencyn was an historical figure whose later life is shrouded in mystery and legend. Descended on his mother's side from Llywelyn Fawr he was a Lancastrian Captain who fought to keep the Yorkist forces out of Nant Conwy but is best remembered as an outlaw and a poet. Numerous tales describe his expertise with bow and arrow and his forcible redistribution of wealth from rich to poor, an activity unlikely to endear him to the house of Gwydir! The

Wynns somehow managed to acquire Dafydd ap Siencyn's spurs which hung for many years in Capel Gwydir (the sole surviving specimen can be viewed on application to the vicar).

9. Ffynnon Gowper stands abandoned and ill cared for. At some time known as Saint Allbright's spring, for centuries this was an important local source of drinking water. Almost two centuries ago it was improved by the Gwydir Estate. Thomas Roscoe recorded the details in his *Wanderings in Wales* (1836), 'At a bowshot from Gwydir Castle stands the fountain of St Allbright. The stream which at this place offers its cooling waters to the lips of the traveller, as it issues through the stone conduit, is supplied by a large cistern constructed for that purpose at a considerable distance up the mountain. An open elevated court, of semi-circular form, stands close to the roadside, backed by a stone wall of corresponding figure, surmounted in the centre by pedimented blocks; a narrow channel perforated in the blocks opens a passage for the pure element, through which it issues all day long in one unceasing stream'. The Estate celebrated the official opening of the fountain with, 'A grand invitation to all the poor old men and women of the neighbourhood, who were plentifully regaled with tea and cakes, and flowing flagons of good ale, and sent merrily home at night with a small portion of money in their pockets'.

Turn right and continue along the road past the Capel Gwydir Uchaf sign to view Gwydir Estate cottages (10) and the entrance to Gwydir Castle (11). A little further on, by the Trefriw road sign, turn left through a sort of open doorway in the wall, ascend the steps and continue to follow the path (12) as it climbs the forestry hillside.

10. One and two Ty'n y Coed and Gwydir Cottage were built in the 19th century to house workers on the Gwydir Estate, and were usually occupied by gardeners. Gwydir Cottage is the earlier example, having been erected around 1845 in a picturesque 'Tudorbethan' style derived from the vernacular architecture of Capel Curig's Tŷ Hyll, known in English as the 'Ugly House'. Although the squires of Gwydir were no longer called Wynn, there was continuity of ownership. In 1678 Lady Mary Wynn had married Robert Bertie, Baron Willoughby de Eresby, who later became the first Duke of Ancaster, and the estate passed down through various Ancasters and de Eresby's until 1895 when it was sold to a cousin, Earl Carrington.

11. This is the main entrance to Gwydir Castle, the historic home of the Wynns (tour is worthwhile, if time permits). The family's great wealth and power and indeed their historical reputation rests largely on the shoulders of Sir John Wynn whose portrait hangs in a lower hall whilst his ghost is said to haunt the spiral staircase leading from the Solar Hall to the Great Chamber. A walled-up void within a chimneybreast is claimed to have concealed the body of a young serving

maid seduced and subsequently murdered by Sir John but such stories lack solid evidence. However history provides numerous well-documented examples of John Wynn's tyrannical behaviour. On his own admission he physically threatened his uncle, Owen Wynn and his tenants following land disputes in Gwydir and Trefriw in 1591. In the same year after a disagreement with William Williams of Cochwillan, his own clansman, he admitted to have given him 'a box on the ear'. Between 1580 and 1611 Sir John Wynn was involved in at least twenty-seven law suits involving fraudulent land transactions, forcible entry, rent abuse and corruption in office. In 1615 he was fined £1,000 for constantly harassing his Llysfaen tenants in an attempt to extract higher rents and it is claimed that he committed a woman to the stocks merely because her son refused to sell him land. Constantly on the lookout for cash he was accused in the Star Chamber of abducting rich widows as rewards for loyal followers and kinsmen, including his own brother, Richard Wynn. After surreptitiously pocketing public defence funds he was warned by the Lord President in 1591 that: 'I wolde have all men know that I do mislike such lewde dealinge'. When Sir John was permitted to purchase a baronetcy in June 1611 he proved reluctant to keep up the payments and by July 1613 was £365 in arrears. Receiving a written rebuke from the Privy Council Wynn nevertheless continued to ingratiate himself at Court and was proud to claim that he had kissed the Prince's hand, dined in the royal household and served as standard-bearer at a royal funeral. Defenders of the Wynns praise the family for continuing to sponsor the age-old bardic traditions of Wales, but for Sir John Wynn they had political value.

Although the Welsh gentry were impatient to become part of the English establishment they were initially careful not to be perceived by their countrymen as having sold out. They retained a foot in both camps whilst it paid them to do so. By the time of Sir John's death in 1627 the Wynns had well and truly 'arrived', and demonstrated little further interest in Welsh culture. Since 1600 an increasing number of poems sung at Gwydir emphasised their patrons' connections with London! For the Wynns and their fellow high-born Welshmen, Union with England offered exciting opportunity; for the ordinary people of Wales it spelt abandonment.

12. This is 'Lady Mary's Walk', named after Lady Mary Mostyn (1585-1653), the daughter of Sir John Wynn. This historic footway connects Gwydir Castle with its summerhouse and pleasure gardens on the hillside above. Despite neglect, the path retains several interesting features including revetting where necessary, steps at the steepest points and slate edging. The forestry may be modern but the path's rather gloomy aspect seems original as it was described in the 17th century as a 'low melancholy walk'.

The path zig-zags up the hillside but stay on course to emerge between Gwydir Uchaf (13), on the left, and Capel Gwydir Uchaf (14), on the right.

13. Although Gwydir Uchaf is an attractive building it was far grander when originally unveiled by Sir John Wynn in 1604. Originally, the Wynn's coat of arms stood above the entrance, surmounting the motto 'Utile Dulci' (Profit and Pleasure)! It is widely

accepted that Gwydir Uchaf was erected to serve as a summerhouse for Gwydir Castle yet historian Mortimer Hart intriguingly suggests that Sir John may have intended it to serve wider political ambitions. Contemporary commentators described Gwydir Uchaf as 'the finest house in Gwynedd', which might add weight to Mortimer Hart's theory that Sir John was actually primarily intent on ingratiating himself with royalty by providing prestigious lodgings for travellers of noble birth or high station journeying to Ireland.

14. Capel Gwydir Uchaf must be viewed internally to be properly appreciated (free admission). Built in 1673 by Sir Richard Wynn (John's grandson) to serve Gwydir Uchaf, services continued to be celebrated here until 1920 with the rector of Trefriw paid a retainer to serve as the Estate's chaplain. The chapel's interior is dominated by a glorious painted ceiling which the Royal Commission on Ancient Monuments claim is 'one of the most remarkable examples of this class of 17th century art in Britain'. Bingley, the 18th century traveller remained curiously unimpressed, 'this is a small building in the Gothic style, sufficiently neat on the outside, but the roof and some other parts are decorated with paintings of scriptural figures, most miserably executed'.

Continue walking to the enormous yew tree in the middle of the forestry yard (16) in front of Gwydir Uchaf and then glance into the nearby walled enclosure (17) now occupied by two modern houses.

15. Much of the area surrounding Gwydir Uchaf was originally laid out as pleasure gardens. The small

hillock just west of the chapel originally formed a low ziggurat or ornamental mound. The term derives from the Babylonian temple-tower design where each tier was smaller than the one below, producing a pyramid effect. The edges of the tiers would be ornamentally planted and it is likely that a pathway ascended the mound, in helicoidal fashion, providing a viewing platform, or mount, as these were all the rage in 16th and 17th century pleasure gardens.

16. This yew tree is a rare surviving example of Gwydir Uchaf's 17th century ornamental planting. The stump situated nearer the building was probably another example. The surrounding car-park area is rubble-revetted to the east and originally provided a viewing platform.

17. Before the forestry insensitively planted these houses in its midst, this was a half-acre walled garden serving Gwydir Uchaf. A variety of soft fruit and vegetables were grown in this sheltered setting and it is quite possible that vines were cultivated here for the production of the wine that records indicate were made by the estate in the 17th century.

Walk down the roadway overlooking Llanrwst on the valley floor to your left, leading in a southerly direction, away from Gwydir Uchaf. Turn first right, past a barrier. After about 80 yards (73m) turn sharp left and follow the forestry track for 600 yards (550m). Just before the main track bears right and turns back on itself you follow a short path to the left to reach a bench (18).

18. This bench marks the position of a Tudor bowling green that originally formed part of the Gwydir Uchaf pleasure gardens, indeed Sir John Wynn mentions playing bowls in a letter to his chaplain. The site was originally selected for its stunning outlook, which provides a particularly good view of the course of the raised walkway (7). Although the bowling-green long ceased to serve its original purpose it continued to be used for festive events by the people of Llanrwst until the years of the Second World War. It was subsequently largely obliterated by the Forestry Commission who drove the track you have just followed through the centre of the green.

Follow the forest lane around the hairpin and the sharp right bend and continue to gently ascend north-west for 500 yards (455m). Where the main track splits, take the smaller right fork track and continue on a fairly level contour until you pick up a series of yellow-topped marker

posts. After 0.3 km the track narrows and soon you are able to see across the market town of Llanrwst and the eastern slopes of the Conwy valley. Follow the path straight ahead, through the two wooden gateways, over the bike track. You begin to hear the sound of running water and notice a parallel path about 70 yards (64m) lower down the hillside on the right. Carry on the path in front. When you reach a junction with another track, bear right and after 55 yards (50m) meet another junction where you turn right down a tarmac path which descends quite steeply. After 165 yards (150m) you turn left along a short footpath which passes a stile on the left and leads into an open, surfaced area (19).

19. Always alert to money-making opportunities Sir John Wynn was eager to profit from the exploitation of local minerals and this was the site of Parc, the largest and longest worked of the Gwydir mines. Mining began here in the early 1600s and only finally ceased in the 1960s. Sir John seems to have first contemplated exploiting local mineral wealth rights in 1611 when he sent two 'great pieces of lead' to the naturalist, Sir Thomas Chaloner, the younger. His researches continued until January 1620 when he leased the mineral rights of the Llanrwst 'wastes and commons' for 40 shillings a year. Failing to extract expected profits, in 1625 Wynn employed a spot of moral blackmail to induce Sir Hugh Myddleton to lend his expertise, 'I beg say to you as the Jews said to Christ, we have heard of they great works done abroad (alluding to the New River and other projects); doe somewhat in thine own country . . . I have lead ore on my ground in great store and other minerals near my house, if it pleases you to come hither'. Although mining continued under the Wynns, it was in the 19th century that Parc expanded dramatically. One noted mining engineer who organised this more systematic approach to extraction was Captain Kneebone, whose name was bestowed on the dramatic cutting situated opposite the information board (accessed via above-mentioned stile). Although most of the workings scattered throughout the forest are 19th century, Sir John Wynn's pioneering role is widely acknowledged and

he is often referred to as 'the father of mining at Gwydir'.

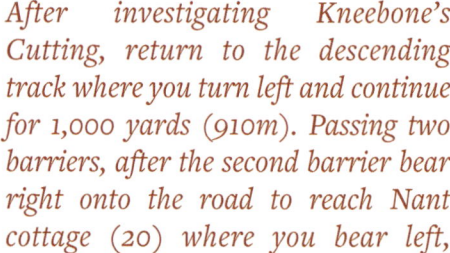

After investigating Kneebone's Cutting, return to the descending track where you turn left and continue for 1,000 yards (910m). Passing two barriers, after the second barrier bear right onto the road to reach Nant cottage (20) where you bear left, following the sign towards Llanrhychwyn, crossing the bridge over the small stream. Cross the ladder stile that soon appears on the right and descend the smaller path down the picturesque gorge, with its waterfalls (21) at the top before crossing a wooden bridge overlooking the curious abandoned ruins (22) at the bottom.

20. Nant was erected in 1845 to accommodate the head forester of the Gwydir Estate, who for much of the 19th century was a man called John White. Although most of the existing forest consists of coniferous trees first planted here in the 1920's (partly by conscripted armies of the unemployed) at the time of the Wynns it was almost entirely oak woodland. This was another resource the house of Gwydir was anxious to exploit. Although a certain amount of timber was sold locally, much of it was floated down river and exported via

Trefriw quay. By the mid 18th century this enterprise alone yielded almost ten thousand pounds a year!

21. This is Rhaeadr y Parc Mawr, also known as the Grey Mare's Tail; but does this particular mare not appear to possess two tails?

22. These are the remains of mill buildings that formerly served two economically important industrial functions for the Gwydir Estate. Felin Blwm was originally erected to crush ore extracted from Parc Mine and could well be the lead mill listed in surviving 18th century estate accounts. Around 1900, with a general decline in lead mining the works were converted into a sawmill and the estate's head forester appointed to also act as timber agent.

Turn left after exiting the gorge area through the large wooden gate and continue along the Trefriw road for 225 yards (200m). Climb over a stone and wooden stile on the right, cross a footbridge over a stream (23) and continue to a wooden ladder stile at the far end of the field keeping with the fence on the left-hand side. Now you follow a delightful lane that provides glimpses across to Gwydir Castle on the right and a little further on an excellent view of the older parts of Llanrwst before arriving at the rear of Tu Hwnt i'r Bont (24). Your original starting point is but a short way beyond.

23. This stream, the lower waters of Nant Gwyd, were intended to become the 'Trefriw Lead Canal'. To facilitate the transport of ore from Felin Blwm (22) to Trefriw quay, for onward shipment, the estate began to canalise the lower waters of Nant Gwyd. The project was seemingly abandoned around 1800, half-heartedly taken-up again in 1820 but never completed.

24. Tu Hwnt i'r Bont was built as a farmhouse in the early 17th century and served as a Court of Sessions under the Wynns of Gwydir. Under the Tudors the responsibilities of Justices of the Peace comprised not only the enforcement of law and order but ensuring conformity to the established religion, the regulation of trade, commerce and employment, the maintenance of the poor and the upkeep of roads and bridges. The partiality and self-interest of the Wynns was renowned and the quality of the justice they dispensed here characterised in verse by Thomas Pennant:

> 'When steel shod cattle crossed the ford
> And the valley ruled by a well-wined Lord;
> I stood a Court House, cold and grave
> As dismal as old Siencyn's Cave;
> On yonder crag I spelt the Law,
> An object of pity, spile and awe
> And many a knarled and trembling hand
> In terror gripped the witness stand;
> As empty-gloried tyrants sat
> And on their fellow mortals spat;
> Their bride-horned justice, dark the day
> Where the Wynns of Gwydir held their sway.'

The Wynns played a key role in the history of Dyffryn Conwy, transforming traditional Welsh patterns of kinship loyalty into hierarchical subservience to the English State. Their enthusiastic anglophile 'modernising' brought the family great wealth and their tenants impoverishment and oppression. Indicted before the Council of the Marches Sir John Wynn, revealing the contempt in which the rising class of Welsh gentry now held their fellow countrymen, dismissed his accusers as, 'illiterate, simple people not having the English tongue'. As Edmwnd Prys, poet and contemporary of Sir John Wynne aptly observed:

> 'Bonedd a fwrian' benyd
> Ar bawb o wrengwyr y byd . . . '
> ('The gentry slaps oppression on all the world's common people . . . ')

Originally published in
Walks in the Conwy Valley

by Christopher Draper

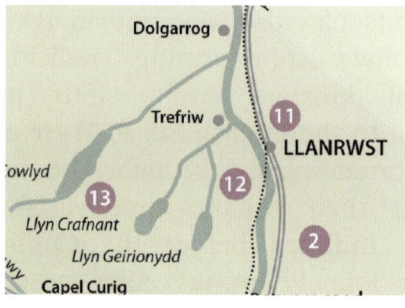

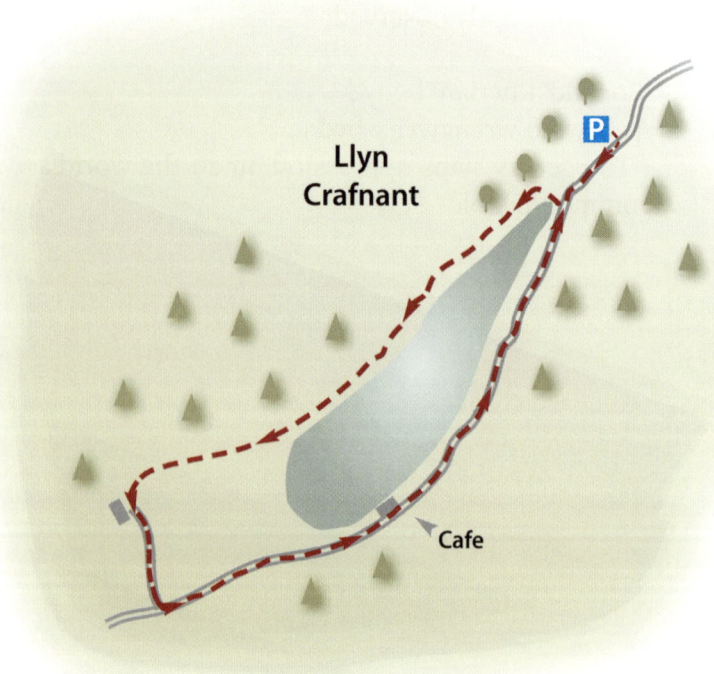

Walk 13
Llyn Crafnant

Walk details

Approx distance: *3 miles/4.8 kilometres*

Approx time: *1½-2 hours*

O.S. Maps: *1:50 000 Landranger Sheet 115*
1:20 000 Explorer OL 17

Start: *Grid Ref. SH 756 618*

Access: *From Conwy, take the B5106 south towards Betws-y-coed. After approximately 9 miles/14.5 km you reach the village of Trefriw. In the middle of the village (before crossing the bridge beside the mill) take a steep and narrow turning off to your right signposted Llyn Crafnant. Follow this narrow road up through the village and continue to follow the signs for Llyn Crafnant. Drive along this narrow lane carefully for about 3 miles/4.8 km until you reach the Forestry Commission car park on your right. There is a very useful information board here.*

Parking: *Forestry Commission car park.*

Please note: *The track is rocky underfoot at the head of the lake.*

Going: *Forest tracks or quiet lanes.*

Site highlights

- Spectacularly scenic mountain and lake views.
- Easy walking up the Crafnant valley with a café en route.
- Woodland birds alongside the track and lane.

Llyn Crafnant

Headline description

This is an easy and enjoyable walk beside the lake following forest tracks up into the base of the cwm at the head of the valley where you will enjoy great views of the hills all around you. The return leg is along a quiet country lane, passing a lakeside café en route. Passing through the woodland bordering the lake in this narrow mountain valley, you may see a mixture of woodland birds, water birds on the lake and Buzzards circling overhead.

Walk directions:

Follow the footpath from the car park, which takes you back onto the narrow lane. Turn right and follow the lane up to the lake (about 200 yards), keeping the fast-flowing Afon Crafnant to your right.

Almost immediately you may be able to hear the high pitched call of Goldcrests in the pines above your head, and you may see Dippers on the stream, feeding on insect larvae and freshwater shrimps.

Immediately before the lake, cross the bridge and go through a metal kissing gate onto the forest track. Follow this track as it continues alongside the lake and at a fork after half a mile (¾ km), take the left-hand track marked with a yellow-top footpath sign, keeping with the lake. You will pass two small waterfalls, and ignore a footpath down to your left which crosses a field after the second waterfall.

The track is lined with berry-bearing bushes, particularly Rowan (Mountain Ash), and pines which provide cover for Coal Tits and Goldcrests, while Stonechats may call from the tops of bracken in the more open areas.

As you reach the head of the lake, the track becomes rockier underfoot and rises uphill slightly. At a yellow marker and footpath sign, take the footpath downhill to your left amongst some large boulders, continue downhill amongst the pine trees. Cross a small wooden bridge over a stream, and emerge on a track by a cottage called Hendre Bach.

The words *hafod* and *hendre* appear frequently in place names in rural Wales. *Hafod* is the 'summer settlement', while *hendre* is the 'home farm', and is usually associated with lowland settlements. These place-names suggest the seasonal movement between high and low level pastures for cultivation and animal grazing.

Turn left along the track, going through the gate and continue slightly downhill past another cottage on your right and a wooden chalet called 'Tan-y-Manod'. At the corner, turn left going through the gate onto a metalled lane. Continue down the valley on the metalled lane, enjoying good views along the length of the lake.

Patches of woodland to the right and left of the lane are worth scanning for views of Treecreepers, while flocks of Long-tailed Tits may pass through. Looking up, Buzzards are often seen circling overhead, while Ravens may pass over. The lake itself does not hold many birds, though Great Crested Grebes, Coots and Mallard are likely to be seen.

After 1 mile (1.5 kilometres) you will pass the Lakeside Café and Tea Garden on your left. Continue back down the lane to the car park on your left.

What to look for ...
... in spring/summer: Check the slopes on the right-hand side of the lake for Tree Pipits. The deciduous woodlands along the lane are a good place to look out for Treecreepers, and keep an eye out too for Redstarts, Pied Flycatchers, Wood Warblers, Chiffchaffs and Willow Warblers in any of the wooded

areas. In spring you will have the added advantage that the birds will be singing, making it easier to locate them.

... in autumn: Redwings and Fieldfares arrive in the area for the winter so you could see these birds anywhere, though they are likely to be attracted to any trees bearing berries. Jays are here all year, but are most obvious at this time of year when they are looking for acorns.

... all year round: At any time of year you are likely to see a Buzzard circling overhead and you should hear its mewing calls echoing off the hills. You may also hear the distinctive 'kronk' of a Raven and see this bird taking advantage of the air currents. Kestrels, Sparrowhawks and Jays are all regulars here, and you may be lucky enough at any time of year to see a Peregrine over the ridges. Check the rushing water of Afon Crafnant as you walk along beside it towards the lake or where  you cross it for Dippers or Grey Wagtails. The lake itself does not hold a lot of bird life, though you should see Mallard and Great Crested Grebes on the water. Goosanders and Red-breasted Mergansers do show up here occasionally. Listen carefully and you may hear the high pitched calls of Goldcrests in the pine trees around the car park, or also in the pine trees around the café. The woodlands at the head of the lake are a particularly good place also to look out for Goldcrests

By the Lakeside Café at Llyn Crafnant

and feeding mixed tit flocks including Coal Tits and Long-tailed Tits, though you may come across them passing through the trees at any stage of your walk. Look out for Stonechats posing on the tops of fence posts or likely bushes. Siskins are often seen and heard high up in the trees around the car park.

Where to eat
The Lakeside Café and Tea Gardens are open mid-March to October, 8 a.m. to 6 p.m., and serving drinks, snacks, homemade cakes and ices. There is limited space inside but plenty of tables outside in the garden overlooking the lake. Rowing boats can also be hired here.

Other information
- Large car park (fee payable) and picnic tables.
- Public toilets in car park.

What other sights are nearby
- Llyn Geirionydd and Gwydir Forest for further walks.
- Gwydir Castle, privately owned and open to the public.
- Historic town of Llanrwst.
- Tourist village of Betws-y-coed.

Originally published in
Birds, Boots and Butties: Conwy Valley/Eastern Snowdonia

by Ruth Miller

Carreg Gwalch Best Walks in the Conwy Valley

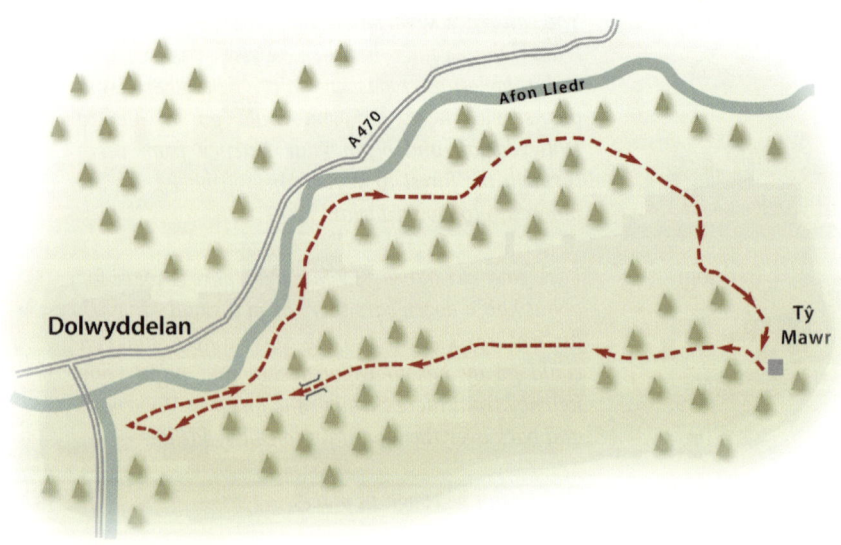

Walk 14
Tŷ Mawr Wybrnant

Walk details

Approx distance: *7 miles/11.3 kilometres*

Approx time: *3¾ hours*

O.S. Maps: *1:50 000 Landranger Sheet 115*
1:25 000 Explorer OL 17 & 18

Start: *Tŷ Mawr Wybrnant*
Grid Ref. SH 770 525

Access: *You can reach Wybrnant either from Penmachno or from the road between Betws-y-coed and Dolwyddelan after passing Fairy Glen. There is no bus service here, but you could go by bus to Dolwyddelan and begin your journey from there through the forest to Wybrnant and back over the mountain to Dolwyddelan.*

Parking: *Park your car outside Tŷ Mawr – there is space for about half a dozen cars there or in a small car park further up. There is no bus service here, but you could go by bus to Dolwyddelan and begin your journey from there through the forest to Wybrnant and back over the mountain to Dolwyddelan.*

Please note: *Tracks can be rough in places.*

Going: *Forest tracks and paths.*

Tŷ Mawr Wybrnant is situated in the Wybrnant valley near Penmachno and was the birthplace of Bishop William Morgan, the translator of the Bible into Welsh.

Tŷ Mawr, Wybrnant

The house has been restored to its probable 16th/17th century appearance and includes a display of Welsh Bibles and Bibles in other languages and an exhibition room. In the house behind Tŷ Mawr is an exhibition on the drovers.

The walk – from yr Wybrant, over the mountain to Dolwyddelan following a possible old drovers' route and then back along the banks of Afon Lledr and through the forest to Wybrant.

Go towards the house called Pwll y Gath (to the right of Tŷ Mawr) – turn left before you reach Pwll y Gath going through gate – and you will see a sign on a post. Follow it to a gate. Go through it and to the left, walking with the wall. Follow the track between two walls to a gate and stile. Go over it and then up the path that goes alongside the wall to a lane. Cross the lane and go straight ahead in the direction of Dolwyddelan. Follow the path alongside the wall to another lane. Cross it and go straight ahead along the path. It can be a bit wet here after heavy rain as with other parts of the path further along.

Go through the trees to a stile. Go over it and to the top of the hill. Follow the path along the flat moorland to a post in the ground and along the path with a large rock on the right. Continue towards another large rock with Foel Felan mountain on your right and keep left and then down towards a stile. Go over it and along the path through the trees. Follow the path through the forest. Continue ahead after crossing a  forestry track. Follow the footpath signs – you will come out of the woods for 300 yards. Keep to the path with a fence and a field on your right. You will then re-enter the forest.

You will come to a lane, turn left going over the stile next to the gate and quarry waste on the left. Go past an old quarry on your left to a gate and kissing gate. Go through the kissing gate and continue along the lane to a fence, gate and kissing gate. Go over the stile, past some houses on the left and to the right and to some bridges. Go over the railway bridge. Turn right and not into Dolwyddelan, but if you have the time  why not pop into the village? There are two hotels – the Gwydir and Elen Castle – and a shop there.

Go to the right past a school and further along Tŷ

Isaf farm and to a gate. Go through 3 gates and walk along the banks of Afon Lledr. Bear left through a gate, keeping with the river. Don't go left over the bridge but keep straight ahead to a gate. Go through it and straight ahead along the wall, past a house on the right to a post in the field and straight ahead until you see a small tunnel on the right. Go through it under the railway and to the left to a stile

Cross the stile and continue along the lane. Go through a smaller gate and past a house on the left and you will see a stile on the right. Go over it and up the field with a stream to your right until you come to a gate. Go through the gate to a lane. Keep left and up the lane, past an agricultural building on the right and then down to a gate and stile. Go over the stile and continue along the lane, ignoring a path that comes up from the left. You will then see a path going to the right. Follow it through the trees, past a post with an arrow on it near a ruin and then straight ahead to a post that points right, up a very rough track and follow it to the left.

You will then reach a post with an arrow pointing to the right, follow it up a steep slope to a post with its arrow pointing upwards. Go through the trees, past four posts to a piece of level ground. Go past another post and through a gap in a wall to a stile and arrow. Go over the stile and keep straight ahead. There is no path now and you will have to walk through long, wiry grass, heather and bilberry bushes.

Go straight ahead with a pine forest on your right (keep within about a hundred yards of the forest).

When you see a deciduous forest in front of you, you will come across a path. Follow it to the left, following a fence until you reach a gate. Go through it and into a field. Go to the right and you will find a gap behind a rock. Go through it and down the field along a poor track and to a bit of path that runs alongside a fence to a gate. Go through it and down through the trees to a small gate. Go through it and past Tan y Clogwyn to a lane. Go to the right and back to Tŷ Mawr.

Bishop William Morgan

A gifted scholar, he studied Hebrew, Greek and Latin at Cambridge University. He was priest of several northern parishes before becoming Bishop of Llandaff and later St Asaph. His greatest contribution was his great work in translating the Bible into Welsh, which he did at the behest of Elizabeth I. He finished the work in 1588 and from then on the Welsh could read the scriptures in their own language. This, say many, is what saved the Welsh language from extinction. The New Testament had already been translated into Welsh by William Salesbury in 1567, but Bishop Morgan's Bible gave the language a formal orthography and a standard written Welsh. His wide vocabulary and the poetry of the translation gave the Welsh a dignified language. Every Sunday, with the royal seal of approval, the Welsh people would hear this dignified language from the pulpits and this was a great contribution to the survival of the language.

Other Points of Interest

Afon Lledr It is a tributary of the Conwy, rising on Moel Siabod and joining the main river just outside Betws-y-coed. It is noted for its salmon and trout fishing.

Dolwyddelan Legend has it that a young woman called Elan, famed for her looks, wished her name and reputation to live forever. She declared: 'Not for nothing am I able to immortalise my name. If there is not any other land prettier than this, henceforth my name shall be upon it.' But the name of the village most probably came from St Gwyddelan, who founded a church here in the 6th century. The present church is reputed to have been built by Maredudd ap Ieuan ap Robert, a distant descendant of Llywelyn Fawr (the Great), who came to live here in the 1500s. Maredudd died in 1525 and is buried in the church, and there is a memorial to him and his family on the north wall of the church.

Dolwyddelan castle It is the birthplace of Llywelyn ap Iorwerth (Llywelyn Fawr). The earliest buildings are early 13th century. The castle covers two routes into Snowdonia, and it remained an important stronghold for his grandson, Llywelyn ap Gruffudd, but its capture by the English – perhaps through treachery – in 1283 was a turning point in the English campaign. It was immediately repaired and garrisoned by Edward I. The English maintained a military presence here until 1290, but their long-term strategy of control relied on military and administrative centres accessible by sea, and inland castles became increasingly irrelevant. The castle was occupied again in the 15th century, when it

Dolwyddelan castle

was leased to Maredudd ap Ieuan, who added an upper storey to the keep.

Drovers The export of store cattle from Wales to the rich pasturelands of England played a vital part in the Welsh economy from the mid-13th century onwards and by the mid-17th century cattle exports were one of the primary sources of Welsh revenue. The growth of urban populations during the late 18th century led to an increased demand for beef and thousands of Welsh cattle were driven into England for fattening after being purchased by dealers and drovers at local fairs. In 1794, 10,000 cattle were exported from Anglesey and by 1810 14,000 were being sent annually to the Midlands from Anglesey and the Llŷn Peninsula alone. Gentlemen employed drovers as carriers of money and news, and Welsh drovers pioneered the establishment of banks in west Wales.

The Welsh drovers who took cattle to London were regarded by the townspeople with suspicion. An account of Barnet Fair in Farmers Magazine in 1856 refers in a rather uncomplimentary fashion to the Welsh drovers: 'Imagine some hundreds of bullocks like an immense forest of horns, propelled hurriedly towards you amid the hideous and uproarious shouting of a set of semi-barbarous drovers ... driving their mad and noisy herds over every person they meet if not fortunate enough to get out of their way ... the noisy "hurrahs" of lots of "un-English speaking" Welshmen ... to be seen throwing up their long-worn, shapeless hats high in the air ... uttering at the same time a ... gibberish which no-one can understand but themselves.'

The size of a drove of cattle varied according to the time of year and demand, ranging from one hundred to four hundred cattle attended by four to eight drovers and their dogs. It took three to four days for the drove to settle down to a steady two miles per hour, a pace which would give the animals opportunity to graze by the wayside. They would cover between fifteen and twenty miles per day so as not to force the cattle and and cause them to lose condition. A long and strenuous day over rough mountain track would be followed by a shorter day's travelling to give the cattle an opportunity to recuperate. The dealer or the foreman drover would ride ahead to arrange accommodation for both men and animals, at either farms or inns, many possessing paddocks where cattle could be held overnight.

The end came with the extension of the railway to Shrewsbury in 1856 and cattle being loaded into railway trucks for the remainder of the journey. Within a few years the railways had reached into Wales enabling the cattle to be carried all the way to the markets.

Originally published in
National Trust Walks 1. Northern Wales

by Dafydd Meirion

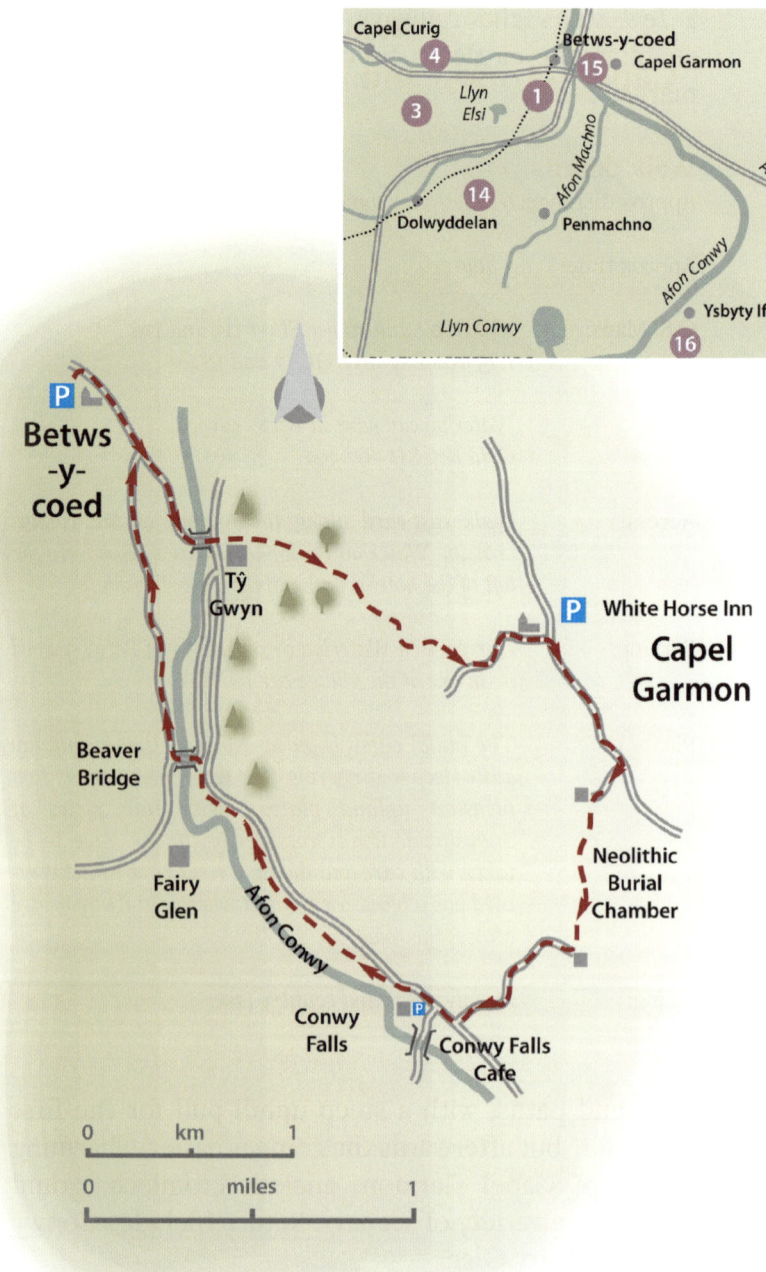

Walk 15
Capel Garmon and its Burial Chamber

Walk details
Approx distance: *6 miles/9.6 kilometres*

Approx time:	*3 hours*
O.S. Maps:	*1:50 000 Landranger Sheet 115 and 116* *1:25 000 Explorer OL 17 and 18*
Start:	*Waterloo car park in Betws-y-coed* *Grid Ref. SH 797 559*
Access:	*Walk eastward along the A5 out of the village, crossing Waterloo Bridge to Tŷ Gwyn Hotel. To the left of the hotel a path climbs the valleyside.*
Parking:	*Car park in Waterloo or on the A5 in Betws-y-coed or in one of the village car parks.*
Please note:	*The initial climb is on an old path that is initially quite steep and narrow. The walk then extends to a pleasant upland plateau with fine views of Snowdonia. Road crossings of the A5 have to be taken with care and the final road back to Betws-y-coed has a blind corner in it where a railway bridge crosses the road.*
Going:	*Mainly paths and country lanes.*

Lane and paths, with a steep uphill pull for the first half-hour, but afterwards the going is easier. Charming village of Capel Garmon, ancient cromlech, grand views and a variety of scenery. Return includes Conwy Falls and Fairy Glen.

Burial Chamber, Capel Garmon

The Walk and Points of Interest

Take a right turn out of Waterloo car park and follow the road over the Waterloo bridge. After crossing, the Tŷ Gwyn Hotel is to your right on the A5. Fifty yards  from the end of the bridge you'll see some stone steps going up from the cottages on the left; they look 'private', but there's a Public Footpath sign by them. Go up the steps, and on up the old path that climbs straight uphill between stone walls, with unyielding steepness. In about 10 minutes you cross a broader forestry track and go straight on for another 5 minutes, through a gate near a house on the left and then on to a tarmac drive. Turn left along the drive for 50 metres and then following the yellow arrow on the wall, turn right through a gap in the wall.

Cross a track, climb over a stile and follow the footpath through some woodland for 150m. Climb a wooden stile into a field by a telegraph pole. Follow the left-hand boundary crossing a low dividing wall to follow the path uphill following a yellow-top pole footpath sign. Continue until you reach the track to Gelli Lynnon farm but do not enter the farmyard. Turn a sharp right at a sharp angle up a grassy track into a field over a wooden stile following the yellow-arrow-top poles. The path across the field is not very clear but keep to your left and soon a kissing gate will come to view ahead of you. Backwards, there are good view of the Glyderau and Carneddau ranges.

A clearer path continues over some rough pasture and joins a farm track. Turn right and pass through the farm yard at Pant y Pwll. These are kennels – don't worry about the dogs barking! Passing between the house and the barn, bear left following the fence through a small wooden gate. The path now curves to cross a wooded gully, crossing the stream over stone slabs and climbing upwards to a stepped stile. Cross an area of rough pasture. You will soon see the village of Capel Garmon in the distance to your left. The track is muddy as it crosses a stream. A large boulder to the right of an open gateway marks the way into the next field. Cross this field heading for the roof of the

farm building ahead. Turn left onto a tarmac lane for the ½ km to Capel Garmon village, joining the main road opposite a chapel.

Turn left if you wish to go to the centre of the village. Capel Garmon village has a delightful air of seclusion and 'out-of-this-world'. It has a compact village centre – the old church, the old post office (both closed now, unfortunately) and the White Horse Inn face each other companionably where the lane twists through between them.

Otherwise, continue on the journey by turning right and follow the road uphill. Pass two kissing gates and a farm entrance to Maes-y-Garnedd as you walk up for ¾ mile/1 km until you see a heritage sign marked 'Ystafell Gladdu Capel Garmon Burial Chamber', pointing to your right.

This is Ty'n-y-coed farm entrance. Follow the farm track and when it curves to your right for the farmyard, go straight ahead to a marked footpath leading through a gate on your left. The burial chamber can be seen towards the left of the next field, secured by a fence from farm animals.

This tomb was built about 5,000 years ago as a tribal burial ground for Bronze Age inhabitants of this area. A long mound of earth would have covered the capping stones of the chamber originally.

Carry on to the left of the chamber and go through a kissing gate and follow the footpath signs pointing left of the rough pasture through the gap in the wall and through the trees. The path rises slightly, with a wall on the right until it joins a farm track. Turn right and follow the track downwards to Penrhyddion farm.

Continue downhill, following the 'diversion' footpath sign. Keeping the fence to your right, you'll come to a wooden stile after 100m. Turn right onto a tarmac road.

Continue along the tarmac track from Penrhyddion farm through two gates with a campsite on your left. Head down the road to the A5, taking care when crossing the busy trunk road, to Conwy Falls Cafe on your right and the entrance to Conwy Falls. Follow the A5 downhill for 150m. The road has heavy traffic at times and there is no footpath. Leave the road at a gap which is the entrance to the old coach road (replaced by Telford's A5 in 1815). Follow the path through woodland with views of the Conwy in a deep gorge to the left.

Passing through gates, the path widens to a comfortable track with views over the Lledr Valley towards Moel Siabod to the left and Dinas Mawr rising to your right. Beyond the fifth gate is the entrance to Fairy Glen.

Continue downwards and join the A470. To return to the centre of Betws-y-coed turn left over Beaver Bridge and immediately right to follow a minor road following the river to your right, where a railway bridge crosses the road. Beware of traffic on the sharp bend.

Back in Betws-y-coed turn right for the Waterloo car park.

Carreg Gwalch Best Walks in the Conwy Valley

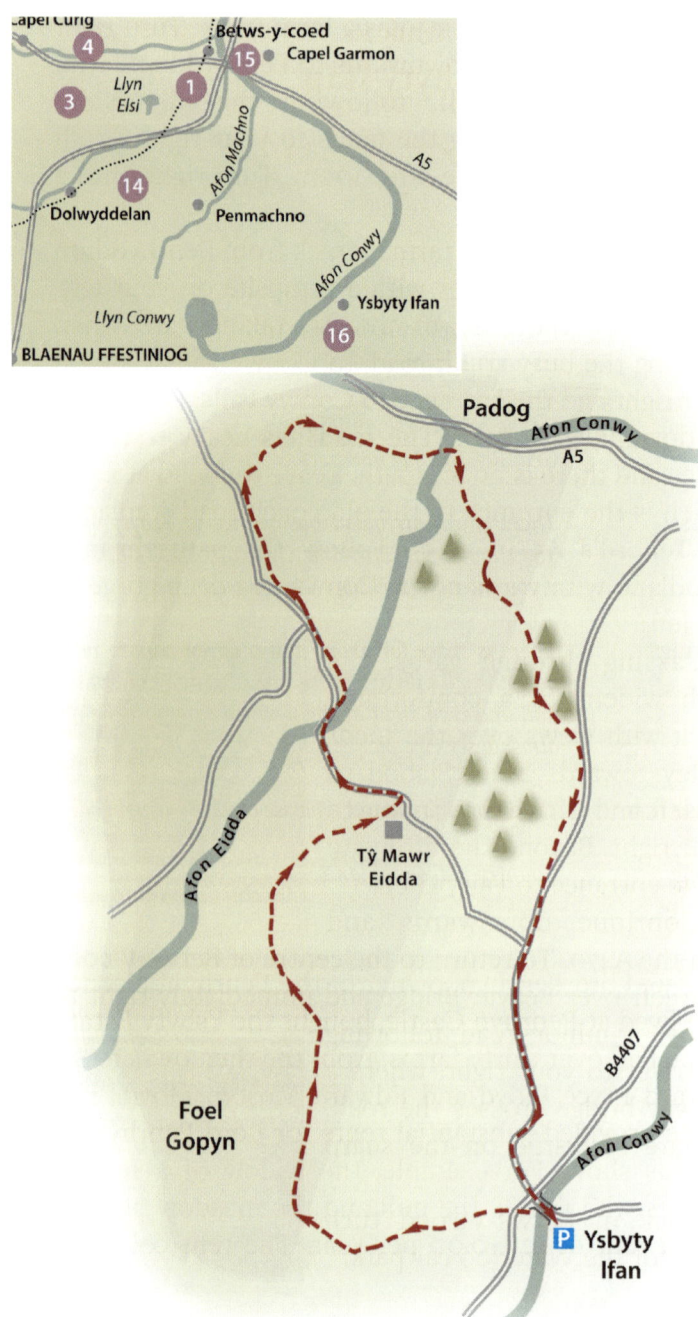

152

Walk 16
Ysbyty Ifan

Walk details

Approx distance: *5½ miles/8.8 kilometres*

Approx time: *3 hours*

O.S. Maps: *1:50 000 Landranger Sheet 116*
1:25 000 Explorer OL 18

Start: *By the bridge, Ysbyty Ifan*
Grid Ref. SH 843 488

Access: *There is an infrequent bus service to Ysbyty Ifan. You should ring Traveline Cymru (0870 6082608) if you intend travelling there by bus.*

Parking: *There is space for about half a dozen cars to park near the old mill at Ysbyty Ifan. Turn left out of the mill and then right at the next turning past the old almshouses (see plaque on the gable end).*

Please note: *Traditional farmland – please abide by usual code.*

Going: *Country paths and lanes.*

In 1856, Lord Penrhyn, owner of the Penrhyn quarries who lived at Penrhyn Castle, bought the Ysbyty Estate which had over thirty farms, from the then owners Sir Edward Pryce Lloyd and Edward Mostyn Lloyd. The estate provided substantial rents for Lord Penrhyn as records show. For example, the widow of a Robert Hughes who rented the mill and the meadow in 1870 paid a rent of £27.10.00 per year. The rent collected

The bridge over Afon Conwy, Ysbyty Ifan

from the whole village – a total of about a hundred farms and homes – was £1,703.13.00, which was a considerable sum for those days.

The National Trust owns and manages the 52 farms which are on the estate today, as well as the old mill.

There is space for about half a dozen cars to park near the old mill at Ysbyty Ifan and a few parking spaces over the other side of the bridge. There is an infrequent bus service to Ysbyty Ifan. You should ring Traveline Cymru (0870 6082608) if you intend travelling there by bus. Turn left out of the mill and then right at the next turning past the old almshouses (see plaque on the gable end).

Go up the hill; don't turn right into the farm but keep straight up along the rough track to a gate. Go through it and proceed along the track to another gate. Go through it and up the track to a lane. Turn right and go along the lane to the crest of the hill and then down, keeping to the lane.

Ignore the lane on the left going to Foel Gopyn and the footpath sign on the right and go straight ahead along the road. Turn right by a gate, follow the track ignoring the stile on your right. Go through the gate next to the cattle grid and follow the lane down the hill. You will come to a farm called Pen-y-bryn, don't enter the farm, follow the lane to the right.

Go through the gate and along the lane to another gate and through the farmyard of Tŷ Nant and then right through a gate, up the lane and to the left, over a bridge and through two gates. Ignore the turning to the right and continue down the hill. Also ignore the stile near the cowshed and go right and up the hill towards Tŷ Mawr. Go through two gates through the farmyard until you come to another lane.

Turn left and down the hill and over the bridge that crosses Afon Eidda. Ignore the stile on the left and go up the hill keeping to the lane, ignoring a lane to the left and right and the lane to Fron Ddu. Then go through the gate towards Bryn Bras on your right. Go along the lane, through a gate, through the farmyard and to the right and along the track through two gates. Cross the stream and down to a gate. Don't go through this gate but go left along the fence to a small gate. Go through it, along the path through the trees with the river on your right, over

the footbridge and out near the A5 close to a telephone kiosk at Padog.

Go to the right to a large expanse of tarmac. To the right is Capel Padog. Follow the path between the garage and the house to a gate. Go through it and up along the wall to a kissing gate and then straight up aiming for two trees and an old wall and a footpath sign. Continue up the slope until you see a farm ahead, aim for a farm. When you reach the fence go to the left and you will reach a stile. Go over it and go to the right towards the farm. You will then reach a footpath sign and a kissing gate.

Go up the field with a forest on your left and to a kissing gate. Go through it and when you have gone

past the trees you will see a kissing gate on your left. Go through it and over a small wooden bridge and to a track up ahead. Go right to the top of the hill through a gate and to a junction. Keep straight ahead to the top of the hill and through a gate and to another gate and junction. Go straight ahead and down the hill and back to Ysbyty Ifan.

Other Points of Interest

A5 Built by Thomas Telford, after pressure to improve the mail service between London and Dublin, work started on this route in 1815. Up until the 1990s it was the main route into northern Wales, connecting with the ferry service to Ireland in Holyhead. The road starts from the Marble Arch in

The old mill, Ysbyty Ifan

London and then follows the old Roman road (Watling Street) to the Welsh border, marked by a bridge over the river Dee. After winding its way through Snowdonia, it crosses the Menai Strait and proceeds along Anglesey to the ferry terminal at Holyhead. The A5 has now been given the status of a Historic Route.

Popty Pen Uchaf The bakery is a venture by one of the tenants of the National Trust's upland farms. Only the best ingredients are used in the traditional recipes and the products are on sale in local shops.

The Old Mill The mill, which was built around 1800, served the neighbouring farms and was an integral part of the village. It is likely that the mill was established on the recommendation of Lord Penrhyn who had the legal right to insist that all the corn grown by his tenants should be ground in his mill. The influence of local mills such as this one in Ysbyty Ifan declined in

The church at Ysbyty Ifan

the early twentieth century with the growth of larger companies in urban areas. By 1940, the last miller, Thomas John Roberts, had started supplementing his income by using the mill to generate electricity for the village. But it was not sufficient for the needs of all the village, and the further from the mill the lower the power. The mill closed around 1960 and in 1997 it became a listed building. The old water-wheel is still behind the mill as well as some of the old machinery inside.

Pen y Bont The village Post Office and Gwniadur are situated in part of the farmhouse. Gwniadur offers a dressmaking, millinery and wedding finery service.

Ysbyty Ifan The original name of the village was Dolgynwal, but it changed when a hospice and garrison was established here in 1190. The *ysbyty* or hospice was established by Hospice Knights, later better known as the Knights of St John of Jerusalem. It became a refuge for travellers and received support from wealthy local landowners and the village grew around it as well as becoming a rich agricultural area. There is a plaque on the present church which is on the site of the old hospice. The knights were given certain exemptions and immunities from the law, so that no officer of the crown could enter their property to arrest lawbreakers. It is said that the immunity was never repealed and the hospice became a refuge for bandits who terrorised the neighbourhood at the end of the Middle Ages.

Originally published in
National Trust Walks 1. Northern Wales

by Dafydd Meirion

First published in 2012

© original authors/Llygad Gwalch

© Carreg Gwalch 2012

All rights reserved. No part of this publication
may be reproduced, stored in a retrieval system,
or transmitted in any form or by any means, electronic,
electrostatic, magnetic tape, mechanical, photocopying,
recording, or otherwise, without prior permission
of the authors of the works herein.

ISBN: 978-1-84524-193-3

Cover design: Carreg Gwalch

Gwasg Carreg Gwalch,
12 Iard yr Orsaf, Llanrwst, Wales LL26 0EH
tel: 01492 642031
fax: 01492 641502
email: books@carreg-gwalch.com
website: www.carreg-gwalch.com

Also in
the
series: